Passport Husband

Marga d'Andurain

Passport Husband

Autobiography

Translated into english by Aurore Julien

Original title : Le Mari Passeport
Firt published in 1947 by Editions Jean Froissart, Paris

PREFACE

Palmyra. Zenobia. Their names alone inspire fantasies and legends. To understand the fascination that the city of Palmyra exerts on writers and adventurers of the nine-teenth century, it is necessary to dive into the history of this oasis of the Syrian desert and its queen Zenobia.

It is very difficult to disentangle the truth from the history of this character of which one ignores almost all. After the death of her husband, Odeinath, Zenobia came to power. She pursues his political ambitions and illustrates herself as a military leader in a context where the Roman Empire is attacked from all sides. She took possession of the Persian territories and then conquered part of Anatolia and southern Lebanon.

In 270, Zenobia controlled all of Egypt and took over the "granary of Rome". She also had coins minted in her effigy. In 272, her domination extends to the whole Anatolian peninsula (current Turkey). When the emperor Aurelian comes to power, he opposes the rise in power of Zenobia in Palmyra. He launched a campaign to reconquer the Empire. Zenobia decided to flee towards the Euphrates but was quickly caught by the Roman soldiers. The end of Zenobia's life is surrounded by many rumors, where myth is mixed with history. Like her birth, the exact circumstances of her death are uncertain. Some Arab sources say she committed suicide to avoid capture. Roman sources claim that Aurelian took her into captivity in Rome, then freed her and she married a Roman senator. Finally, other sources claim that she was beheaded in Palmyra.

Zenobia, has captured the imagination of generations of writers, fascinated by the exploits of this powerful queen who managed to defy Rome. She brought the city of Palmyra into posterity. Known as the "Pearl of the Desert", the oasis city was renowned for its magnificent buildings, such as its Triumphal Arch and its impressive theater. In the 18th century, some European travelers began to venture into these places and revived the memory of Zenobia, the sumptuous queen of Palmyra. From the stories of their discoveries, they will give birth to a thirst for adventure, a desire for the East in the future generations of adventurers. The daring Russian Lydie Paschkoff, had visited Palmyra in 1872, before publishing in *World Tour*, an account of her trip both colorful and full of observations : "For a long time I wanted to see Palmyra. The ruins of this city, once splendid, now buried in the desert, the history of its prosperity, its capture by the Romans, the fall of Zenobia its last queen, (...) all this romantic set attracted me to the country where so many interesting and tragic events had taken place".

When Lady Hester Stanhope arrived in Palmyra in 1813, delighted with the welcome she received from its inhabitants, she wrote to a friend : "I was crowned Queen of the Desert under the triumphal arch of Palmyra. Nothing was as successful as this journey, which seemed so dangerous. Everyone paid tribute to me. If I wanted to, I could go to Mecca by myself. I have nothing to fear." The indomitable English aristocrat eventually never made it to Islam's holy city and settled in the mountains of Lebanon where she died in misery. A century later, in 1933, Marga d'Andurain was about to go on a pilgrimage to Mecca. If, like Lady Hester, the Countess had pro-claimed herself "Queen of Palmyra", she did not identify herself with her : "I am neither Lady Hester Stanhope nor Lady Jane Digby. These noble English women of the nineteenth century wanted to end their days in the arms of a Bedouin lover. Not in my case, I have a husband who approves of my conduct and the only thing I desire is my freedom".

Marga intended to undertake a journey of extra- ordinary magnitude, she was not unaware of the dangers she would face. As in the nineteenth century, European travelers in disguise who were discovered in Mecca and the surrounding holy places risked irreparable death. All of them, without exception, were taken out of the holy city to the nearby desert, beheaded and buried in unmarked graves. In the past, only two women had made it across the Neyed's lonely and threatening black sandy desert, and with great difficulty. Lady Anne Blunt, granddaughter of the poet Lord Byron, became in 1879 the first European woman to cross the deserts of central Arabia in search of thoroughbred horses for her stables in England. In her book, *A Pilgrimage to Nejd*, Lady Blunt recalls the terrible experience of crossing one of the world's harshest and most extensive deserts : the camels collapsed from heat and exhaustion, disobeyed her orders and refused to carry their luggage; without food or water, they nearly lost their lives. For her part, the famous diplomat Gertrude Bell braved the hell of the reddish dunes whipped up by sandstorms to reach the forbidden city of Hayil in northern Arabia. The motives that led the Countess of Andurain to undertake such a reckless and dangerous adventure are one of the many mysteries that surround her life. She wanted to write a book about her adventure in Mecca that would undoubtedly make her famous throughout the world. Marga, not satisfied with being the only European woman able to live in Palmyra, driving alone in her car on dangerous desert tracks and hanging out with Bedouins in their tents, wanted to do something that no one of her gender had ever done before.

Marga d'Andurain's personality is the subject of much discussion. Whether one sees in this beautiful, elegant, sporty and worldly woman, an adventurer, a spy or even a scatterbrain who always got herself into impossible situations, there is one point on which everyone agrees : Marga d'Andurain had everything to fire the imagination. It is not surprising, in these conditions, that the press did not fail to embroider on her life and her death. The rocky and mysterious life of Marga is punctuated with adventures often troubled. In the evening of her life, she will have inherited several nicknames given by journalists: "the Queen of Palmyra", "the Mata Hari of the desert", "the Countess of the twenty crimes", "the mistress of Lawrence of Arabia", "poisoner", "spy and double agent" for the account of the English and then of the Arabs... or again, trafficker in pearls, opium and gold, nymphomaniac, drug addict... the list increases as the character disappears from the memory of her contemporaries to enter another category of analysis, that of the fantasy of the adventurous woman. Her journey was sufficiently unusual to arouse interest, as had been the case with other adventurers before her, Isabelle Eberhardt, Ida Pfeiffer, Alexandra David Neel or Ella Maillard. But having played no official role, having written little, she left few traces. Dressed in Western or Arabic style, fully claiming the power to act like men, she embodied this "desire for the East", which had animated some Western women of the early twentieth century.

Marga d'Andurain published "Passport husband" in 1947, one year before her death. She recounts her adventures in the Middle East. In 1927, Marga and her husband, Pierre d'Andurain, settled in Palmyra in Syria, where they bought a hotel, which Marga renamed Zenobia in honor of the fascinating queen of the third century. There, two chance meetings led her to plan the great adventure of her life, a project that is difficult to describe : audacious, reckless, dangerous, a little crazy ! It was to be the first western woman to enter the holy city of Mecca to participate in the annual pilgrimage. But not everything goes according to plan. The "Passport husband" recounts the singular, and sometimes painful, adventures she experienced during this trip to Saudi Arabia, in order to refute the accusations she was subjected to during this journey. The twists and turns are intertwined at a steady pace and the unspoken facts are as numerous as the probable affabulations. Marga d'Andurain was the architect of her own legend.

Marga d'Andurain at the time she wrote
"Passport Husband"

TO MR. ROGER MAIGRET MINISTER OF FRANCE IN THE KINGDOM OF NEDJ, HEDJAZ AND YEMEN TO WHOM I OWE MY LIFE.

INTRODUCTION

WHY WRITE, WHEN YOU DON'T KNOW how to write ? Why talk about oneself for three hundred pages when the self is hateful ?

Because all the French and foreign press, after announcing my death by hanging, told incredible things about me.

Because, following certain coincidences and in a total incomprehension of my acts, the General Security and the Intelligence Service of Syria built on my account an abominable file, which ruined me morally and financially, and of which I cannot obtain the communication, but that many of my relations in Paris, and even the Basque deputy of the Basses-Pyrénées, boast to have seen at the Foreign Affairs, spreading the most slanderous comments about me.

The only interest of this story, in my opinion, is that everything I say is absolutely true, all the people mentioned in this book live (except the passport husband), are in place and I name them.

I challenge them all to be able to deal with an inaccuracy.

This story has no pretensions, it does not sacrifice to any prejudice, any ulterior motive, any diplomatic or selfish precaution. It tells what I saw with the maximum precision possible.

And I would like finally - it is a simple wish - that one would forget a little, after reading me, the slanders and nonsense piled up, with passion, around my acts and my name.

13

Will I be understood, as I was as a child, as I lived the events I relate, as I remain at this hour ?

CHILDHOOD

I WAS BORN IN BAYONNE, TO A BASQUE family on the strain from which I come from, generations of worthy bourgeois, magistrates, notaries, soldiers, civil servants have come. There have also been gentlemen living on their lands, carrying the sword or born to distant diplomatic labors.

It is well known that in all Basque people there are distant hereditaries of adventure seekers. We have an obscure origin that neither ethnologists nor linguists have yet been able to specify. Why does the distant soul of the Basques, runners of the seas and continents, after so many centuries when the beings of my blood had ignored that it could still ferment in them, think of being reborn in the little girl promised to all the monotonies of provincial life, that I was born and had to give up ?

It began with childish testimonies. For example, my embarrassment and the secret protest of my whole being when I had to obey orders that I did not admit.

I was attracted to the work by a strong need to know. Only, in addition, a no less ardent desire for independence was developing. Judge for yourself : when I was three years old, I was running away from my parents' house one day. I wanted to go out alone. I felt proud to pass in front of a sentry who guarded the old Bayonne gunstock. I went to hide under a bridge where I felt freer, leaving my family in a panic for a whole day.

Another day, later, having taken my sister's bicycle on a towpath, I wanted to perform feats that my little legs did not allow and I fell into the Gave river.

Of course, these fantasies, and many others, were carried out in spite of family prohibitions and in a kind of disdain for the danger that I had guessed so well. However, I was growing up, and with me my "faults".

My family was setting an example of a quiet and peaceful life that I began to abhor. The rituals of propriety, the receptions, the exchanges of visits, the hypocritical politeness, the kindness followed by gossip without gentleness, everything that is the basis of provincial existence, made me nauseous.

Soon I could not curb my tastes or the manifestations of my indiscipline. The docility with which, in spite of everything, I often testified, gave way to a violent insubordination. It was necessary to consider the best way to put an end to this childish anarchism. They decided to put me in a convent when I was nine years old.

Alas ! Educators hardly conceive of reducing non-conformist minds through persuasion, gentleness, kindness. We rely on force, which however seems to have gone bankrupt. It was not to succeed with me.

I already had and still have, to the highest degree, a great need for truth, accuracy and honesty. It fitted well with the advice I was getting from everywhere, but not with the way it should be understood. I was called St. John the Golden Mouth for my brutal sincerity.

My education was entrusted to all possible religious orders in France and Spain. From each establishment, revolt, impertinence and what is called dissipation soon made me dismissed.

Note that I was neither lazy nor a bad student. The only time I spent the entire school year in one of these convents, I received all the class prizes, except for the wisdom prize. I went home with piles of golden volumes, a laurel wreath like an empress and the kind embrace of Monseigneur Gieure, Bishop of Bayonne, who had come that day to preside over the distribution of the prizes to the Ursulines of Fontarabie.

I mention this event because it was exceptional. Everywhere else, before july came, I was put on emergency duty, either for having scandalously violated the rule, or for having fomented revolt in a dormitory, or for a crazy escape according to my tastes. My family, discouraged by so many former impulses, wanted to try an education at home. I was entrusted to a teacher.

But, during the vacations, I met again in Biarritz my cousin d'Andurain who had left the country a few years ago. I liked him immediately, I invited him to the countryside, our marriage was decided between us. My father objected to my extreme youth, the instability of my character, my absolute lack of experience,

practicality and... Pierre d'Andurain had no situation.

My dear mother fought to get my father's consent. It was then that I saw my future mother-in-law; the interview took place at other cousins' home.

For this reception, my hair was set in a bun and I wore one of my cousin's long dress, so that my mother herself almost didn't recognize me, as I was so bundled up to look older. As soon as the interview was over, I took back my short skirts, relaxed my hair and went back to my usual exercises which were horseback riding and climbing trees.

Finally after six months of struggle and objections my parents allowed my marriage.

SPYING

MY HUSBAND SHARED MY TASTE FOR TRAVEL, new skies and suns. We immediately wandered through Spain, Portugal, Morocco and Algeria, stopping wherever we wished.

In 1912 we returned to France and left for South America. I hate cold, foggy, unlit countries. I need the scorching sun. In 1914, the war brought us back to France. My husband left for the front. Enveloped by the explosion of a shell in front of Verdun, he was discharged in 1916; his health now prevented him from leading the vagabond existence of yester years.

Our fortunes, by the way, were significantly diminished. We had to find funding. I was told of a Swiss man who made expensive artificial beads for his industry, both as an orderer and a local. Talks took place, we got along, and the Swiss settled in a large workshop that I lived in, 29, avenue Henri-Martin.

So here I am making beads, but my partner's process was primitive. I wanted to do better, so I started on my own, and with the help of a skilled and well-known chemist, we created a very perfect pearl, flawless mother-of-pearl and a beautiful orient. My business grew to a size I didn't expect, but since I only sold wholesale, most of the profits went to middlemen.

Since, on the other hand, my family would have been shouting if I had opened a sales store, I decided to leave.

Since my father had died in the meantime, my mother tried to get us to come back to her so that we would give up making money from a business that she felt was shameful. But it was in vain.

The allure of a rich country, where the sky is pure, the sun warm, was not one we could resist. One fine day, in Marseilles, we took with our furniture the liner of Egypt.

I didn't really think I was on my way until the boat had left the ground. Obstacles arose, until the last moment, in front of my eagerness to leave.

The bell had rung, the siren had torn the air, but I was alone on board with my two children and my eyes were scanning the swarming dock where my husband did not arrive. At last he appeared, perched on a truck carrying our twenty-five trunks. He was taken for the impresario of the Clara Tambour tour... Ah ! this departure, what a sigh when the propellers turned !

But after an uneventful trip, what a drama in Alexandria; the customs, for a signature affixed without thinking, at the bottom of a printed form, and this at the very moment when I was scrupulously writing down what we had to declare, claims to impose a fine of one hundred thousand francs on me ! Eight days of negotiations and the intervention of the French Consul spared us this ruin, but the incident did not leave us free of a very high price. A little later, we were installed in Cairo, in a brand new apartment, in front of the famous Groppi. We had to work, but the success was immediate.

I spent two winters in the city and the summer at the San-Stefano sea baths. We went out, we frequented the Sporting-Club, my husband rode horses there. Why, one will ask, did I only stay there for two years ? Because my passion for change took me to other places.

I met in Cairo the Baroness Brault, English by birth, who told me one day about a trip she was going to make to Syria and Palestine with an officer of the Intelligence Service of Haifa and another English woman also, the Honorable Mrs. Mead, goddaughter of King Edward VII. This one being sick at the last moment, I took her place with joy, despite the warning of a friend who warned me against my too close relations with the English and predicted that such a trip would give me a file. I burst out laughing, this advice seemed unbelievable to me. I left for Haifa and visited Palestine with the Major S. and Mrs. Brault. We ended up in Damascus, where we had the opportunity to travel to either Palmyra or Baghdad. Major S.'s leave was about to expire and we could not do both. The Baroness preferred Baghdad, for me, I was naturally more concerned about the fabulous site of Palmyra lost in a desert, then less accessible than today.

My insistence prevailed and we left for those ruins. The impression I got from it was great. This immense field of golden ruins. These rows of columns lost in the sand, these boundless horizons, this palm grove whose dark green contrasted with the empty expanse of the desert, and, above all, this solitude, this silence, this life that seemed to be that of another world, made me understand right away that I had discovered the home of my dreams. As soon as I arrived, I felt like a child of this strange land and decided to settle there to set up a breeding farm as I had done in South America. All I had to do was convince my husband. So I returned to Cairo and convinced him without any difficulty.

Fifteen days later he preceded me in Palmyra. During this time, I was liquidating my Egyptian business. I went to Greece to shoot a short film.

Then I went to Italy, and finally to France, where I went to attend the First Communion of my youngest son, which took place in the Cathedral of Bayonne, but my fidelity to the AF, the nationalist and royalist party, made me refuse absolution and I could not accompany my son to the holy table. This was at the time of the drama between the AF and the Vatican.

There I received some extremely surprising news from my husband. He had been received in Palmyra, and in the most cordial way, by the small group of officers of the position, partnered with them, shared their life, was treated as a comrade by them, in his quality of reserve officer.

But a certain Colonel Ripert, who was then in command at Deir-ez-Zor on the Euphrates and on which Palmyra depended, thought it good to be surprised that I had come to Palmyra with Major S... , feared and frowned upon by the Frenchman. So he asked me to stop seeing him and especially not to return with him to Syria under any pretext.

I fell from the sky ! Who was I to receive advice, almost orders from a colonel ?

As I have been forced to say a hundred times since then, I am only a private person, a stranger to the army, and I feel free to associate with whomever I please.

I had agreed to see Major S. again in Palestine and saw no reason to change my plans. So I returned to Cairo to pick up my eldest son and went to Haifa. When I passed through Kantara, the Palestinian authorities stripped me of my gun and sent it in transit to the border.

I went to Haifa, to the home of Major S..., and he, my son and I left for Damascus. I tried to recover my revolver, but as it had not arrived, we found it useless to wait, so I gave my papers to the major to recover it later, and he lent me a revolver of his in the meantime.

That same evening we had dinner in Damascus where, two days later, I left the major, leaving at dawn with my son to join my husband in Palmyra and we settled in a hut in the village. A few days later, I was visited by English friends who had come to

Cairo...

The mediocrity of the few officers I dealt with seems even more lamentable today, when I think about it. My relations with Major S..., imbued with that simple comradeship, so pleasant and sympathetic, which attracts me so much to the English, and which most French people do not even conceive of, anchored in these tiny minds the fixed idea that I had come to Palmyra to study its serious military secrets and to deliver them to the enemy for a large sum of money. The visit of my English officer friends reinforces this opinion that an ounce of common sense should have been enough to dispel. If the object of my stay in Palmyra had been espionage, would I have chosen to go there with the head of the Palestine Intelligence Service ? Would I have been visited there immediately by officers of the Egyptian army ? And when, a few days after my arrival, I was robbed of the major's revolver, would I have gone to complain to Captain Bottle, who was then in command in Palmyra, telling him with candor who the owner of the weapon was and offering to write to Haifa to find out his factory number, which he asked me to do in order to facilitate the search ? But it is probably useless to wonder why such silly ideas germinate in some brains.

Anyway, the gossips were making their way and doing it without my knowledge. While waiting for the response of the estate administration to my request for land for my livestock projects, my husband and I began to build a small house on the edge of a warm water spring, in a pretty garden that belonged to Sheikh Abdallah, the master of the village of Palmyra, famous for having been kidnapped by Mrs. Perouse, niece of President Grévy.

This old man was still recounting his memories of Chenonceaux and the Opera. We lived there six months of administrative slowness. One fine day, the officers of the post, with whom we had frequent and cordial relations, told me that a Comptroller of the army was coming. By the greatest of chances, this officer, the Comptroller

General Péria, happened to be my relative and the prospect of this unexpected meeting in the village amused me a lot. However, he didn't show up and it was quite by chance that I ran into him a few days later in a hotel in Damascus.

He seemed rather embarrassed to meet me, but the family solidarity probably won out because he took me aside for a confidential interview. What he told me was astonishing. At first, he was content to commit me to leave Palmyra and return to France, the only country where one can live honestly. As such an advice could not have any meaning for me, he was forced to tell me more and I found out that I was passing for a female spy, that I had an awful record, that it was assumed that my presence in Palmyra had no other purpose than to facilitate my meeting with the formidable Major Sinclair and a thousand balderdashes of the same quality. In addition, my relative added, I could return to France since Major Sinclair had died. I was stunned, and my astonishment at this news, which I did not know, still seemed a comedy to this unfortunate cousin, who nevertheless left me, giving me an appointment for the next day in Beirut. So I went there and did everything I could to provoke a decisive explanation at the High Commission; I heard the most unlikely things.

It was in the intelligence service of the High Commission that the famous raports that caused all my troubles were concentrated. It appears then that the whole machination was orchestrated mainly by Colonel Ripert. This officer, whose misogyny was well known (Palmyra was forbidden to the wives of soldiers), had no doubt been ill-disposed towards me from the beginning. One remembers the words he had said to my husband.

Possessed, like so many Frenchmen of Syria, by a sickly Anglophobia, by a mania to see the hand of England in the most insignificant events and in those where the interest of England is most obviously absent for a thoughtful officer, he had charged two snitches to report to him on my activity in Palmyra.

A certain Felix, who had only come out of obscurity until then, for a few convictions under common law, had been employed in a hotel that a consortium had organized in Palmyra... Business had been poor, exploitation was poor and discord arose between the parties of the consortium, each of which refused to become the owners again. Felix, taking advantage of this troubled situation, remained, usurping the title of guardian, to squander the furniture and silverware. One could believe that the officers of the intelligence service, who did not miss an opportunity to express their contempt for this individual, kept him at a distance.

But no. Felix treated them as comrades, joined them as if he had been at home and gave them all sorts of reports. On the other hand, a sieur Lakache, known as Joubert, representing the Security agency in Palmyra, was one of Felix's closest friends.

I found out at the High Commission that these two honourable comrades had been asked by Colonel Ripert to provide reports about me. It goes without saying that these reports responded to the wishes of the colonel, they continued precisely the kind of documentation that our snitches thought would please him. We know the mentality of the junior agents of the Security agency, and as for Ripert, during five years in Syria, I never met an officer who did not despise him. Moreover, he was involved in high-profile trials in which he confessed to committing forgeries. This is the quality of my enemies.

The colonel was therefore served abundantly and passed on to Beirut the gossip of his brilliant informers, giving them the weight of his authority. To conclude, he demanded my expulsion.

The report was transmitted to Colonel (since General) Catroux. As there is never a funny element missing in these matters, Colonel Catroux received, by the same mail, a note from Marshal Lyautey who recommended us to him...

One will wonder what was in those unfamous reports. I would like to be able to say it, but all of my requests for information never succeeded, neither in Paris nor in Beirut. I only obtained from the Comptroller General Peria the following details: I was reproached for the relations I had had in Cairo with the Lotfallah princes, whose role in Syrian politics is well known ; the anti-French propaganda I had allegedly made in Baghdad; my relations with Baroness Brault, an unofficial agent of the Intelligence Service, whose company was even more compromising, as my poor cousin said, than that of the famous Gertrude Beil.

In addition, how can I explain the fact that my husband and I, although we had a business in Cairo, were members of the Sporting-Club ?

Wasn't that the clue to my occult relationship with the Intelligence Service ?

It will probably be considered unnecessary for me to respond to these last two grievances. As for my propaganda in Baghdad, suffice it to say that, even today, I have never set foot in that city, nor in any other city in Iraq. As for my relations with the Lotfallah, I had been linked by my affairs, and then by a real sympathy, to Princess Michel who had helped my beginnings in Cairo and whom I found to be charming. But when it came to political matters, my conduct was quite different. It was I, in particular, who, invited to lunch in Cairo by the Duke of Orleans, dissuaded him from seeing the Lotfallah brothers, who, on three occasions, telephoned during the meal to obtain his presence at their hunts or receptions. The Duke, following what I told him, cancelled an audience which he had granted them, declaring forcefully that he did not admit to seeing an enemy of France.

Dr. Récamier was a little annoyed, at the time, to cancel this hearing. It was the last trip of the Prince who died twenty days later in Palermo and here are, to confirm what I said, some extras from the letters that my husband received from Dr. Récamier, the Prince's doctor :

"1, rue du Regard, May 23, 1926.

Dear Sir,

You are certainly the last French people that Monseigneur received at his table and perhaps the last people that the Prince spoke with outside of his servants.

Although I was concerned at the time of our visit to Cairo, as I saw the Prince sad and tired from the exhausting journey, I had no idea how dangerous it was. He had been vaccinated the year before and I confess that the fear of a hypertoxic smallpox was the least of my worries.

However, it is in Cairo or Alexandria, almost without leaving the hotel, that he had to contract the disease."

In January 1928, he wrote to us again :

"Your visit to the Prince, in Cairo, had given him great pleasure; thanks to the courageous and very French cheerfulness of Madame d'Andurain, he spent happy moments with you, as he does every time he met French people whose devotion he felt. But the Prince owed you much more than a moment of calm and moral rest, you did him the greatest service by enlightening him as you did on the true personality, the true tendencies of this Lotfallah, who sought to penetrate his intimacy. For my part, I have always been grateful to you for this.

I do not forget either the tribute that the French colony in Cairo paid him after his death, thanks to your initiative.

Please, dear Sir, offer my most respectful homage to Madame d'Andurain and believe in my very devoted feelings.

L. Recamier. "

The ineptitude of the grievances with which I was charged should have been evident, it seems, of a department with some pretension to critical thinking. It was not so. The spectre of English espionage provoked the same obsession in Syria as that of German espionage in France during the war. One could write a book on this disease, for which there are few cures.

In any case, I found out during these same interviews that a helpful person, I could never know who, had the odious idea of bringing these accusations even before my mother, an elderly woman, of a burning patriotism, closely confined to the ideas of another generation and in whose eyes, as in mine for that matter, no crime could seem more monstrous. I understood immediately what a terrible shock these accusations must have been for her and I obtained that a dispatch was sent to her at once, the content of which was submitted to me, giving sufficient proof of the sense in which the authorities were in their scandalous misunderstanding. He said, verbatim : "Big mistake, a matter admirably finished".

In addition, Colonel Arnauld, Colonel Catroux's successor at the head of the Intelligence Service, addressed the following letter to my husband :

GENERAL SECRETARIAT INFORMATION SERVICE
Beirut, December 19, 1927.

Sir,

I would like to assure you once again that you are not under any special surveillance and that all instructions have been given so that you and Mrs. d'Andurain can live in peace and confidence in Palmyra. I have no doubt that in this way, with everyone's good will, any incident will be smoothed out.

However, I would ask you to recommend to Mrs. d'Andurain to be very careful in her relations with foreign persons, so as not to give rise to suspicion in any subordinate agent. I am giving you this advice because I know that the Comptroller, your relative, has already given it to Mrs. d'Andurain.

Thinking that these few lines will give you peace of mind, I send you, Sir, my greetings and ask you to believe in my distinct feelings.

The Director of the Intelligence Service in the Levant,

Colonel ARNAULD

And, so that the reparation was complete and public, the military authorities of Palmyra received the order to file at the door of the seraglio and posted, indeed, a note which said in substance : "The d'Andurains are perfectly honourable French people, to whom one has nothing to reproach. The soldiers are asked to be respectful with them".

The only practical result of this explanation was to rid Palmyra of Lakache and Felix. The first was removed without drum or trumpet, it seemed to be realized that a post of the Sûreté did not really answer to anything to Palmyra and it was suppressed. As for Felix, I asked him to leave too, alleging his false reports. The content of these reports, as I said, was and still is unknown to me. But their slanderous character was at no time contested by the authorities with whom I had to discuss them. The departure of Felix was therefore decided, as a matter of principle. However, the hotel was to remain empty. This seemed to me to be an insignificant matter, especially since Felix had not been given the task of guarding the building by anyone. I don't know why, the authorities seemed to fear this abandonment. I lifted this difficulty by proposing to them to take over the management of the hotel myself, which was done.

One fine morning, Felix left Palmyra. His departure even took the comical form of a clandestine kidnapping, whose adventures, to tell the truth, have no place here.

So my husband, my eldest son and I moved into the hotel. A few years later, when the consortium was liquidated, I became the owner and still own it. Those years could have been easy and, in terms of running the hotel, profitable.

But I found all the administrative obstacles that had repelled the first owners and I also encountered a thousand difficulties from the two information offices of the three that followed during my stay.

One of them was a simple crook, and I am currently pro-secuting him for swindling several thousand francs. The other, incomparably worse, shameless scoundrel, soon became my mortal enemy and swore that he would have my skin. So I was not surprised the evening when my room was attacked at night by a well-chosen gang of armed men who ran away in the face of resistance they had not foreseen.

The bullets that I missed were picked up, in my room, an iron baton, which had also fallen in the fight, was seized; bare footprints were found on the tiles that had been polished the day before, but that was of no use and the case was hushed up after an investigative comedy.

BEDOUIN EPISODES

AS SOON AS WE WERE INSTALLED IN OUR small house, we received frequent visits and endless invitations from Arabs. I liked these people, so different from us, and I soon found real joy in the visits I made myself to the black tents that the Bedouins carried from place to place, in their slow transhumance through the desert.

The generous hospitality of these nomads, their extreme politeness, the sense of honor so developed in them, quickly made us forget the differences that could have separated us on other points. When I arrived at the camp, surrounded by camels in the pasture, I went to the tent of the Sheikh, always easy to recognize, thanks to his dimensions. I greeted the sheik, holding my hand to my forehead, and crouched like all the men present, next to the fire where the long-spout coffee and teapots were lined up. A man would grind the coffee in a mortar and rhythmically pace his work, and we would drink the well-boiled, unsweetened and fragrant infusion of a few cardamom beans in small cups without handles.

At night, came the "kassoud", improvised poet, whose recitation was commented by an expressive mimic. Then I passed under the women's tent, where the children were swarming. I fell asleep there, all dressed, on a few blankets, protected by a screen of rushes joined together by multicolored threads.

Sometimes the sheik would come and make sure that I was well covered and tucked me in paternally. When I woke up, I would be poured into a wooden bowl some camel milk, which, according to my hosts, was a sign of strength and health. In the calm of this simple life, I tasted a deep inner satisfaction that I cannot express, but that civilized life has never given me.

From time to time, the distraction of a hunt varied existence. Bedouins still often hunt hares and bustards with falcons. Gazelle hunting, on the other hand, is almost always done by car, now that the Bedouin chiefs all have cars. I have often participated in it, notably at Sattam's, sheik of the Hadidins.

It needed a solid car ! I sat in the front seat, between Sattam and his black driver, while six Bedouins piled up at the back of the car, in their ample draped clothes. And we were cutting down the kilometers until someone shouted: "Gazellan, gazellan ! »

As soon as the gas pedal is pressed, each one arms his gun, it is a moment of confusion in the car which leaps up more and more beautifully, in defiance of the clods and tufts of dried grass. At a hundred and ten an hour we arrive in the middle of the herd, and the light animals launch themselves into a desperate flight, their thin legs seem to barely carry them, they fly, without ever leaving us with their immense pathetic black eyes. But no pity, we shoot. Their short black tail is like a target, in the middle of their white buttocks. Several are wounded, but do not want to leave the herd. It is only when they are completely exhausted that they fall down. We continue to pursue, to shoot, until we see nothing more on the horizon.

An old male is still running; one of his broken legs, almost cut by a bullet, seems to be held only by a tendon, but he is still running, bleeding. I feel my heart tightening for a moment and I would like to finish him off. But another leg is broken and he goes back to fall. He raises his big black eyes, and in the excitement of the massacre we run to cut his throat, according to the Arab rite, and then we return to our tracks to pick up the forty or so victims that we have sown there. Other animals, no doubt, were able to flee and, wounded to death, went to some corner of the desert to be devoured by foxes, hyenas and jackals.

But the evening comes. We are too hungry to wait for the return to the camp, and it is not the game which misses.

We skin some gazelles. A quickly flaming can of gasoline will make the pot, and camel dung will make the best fuel. Gazelle quarters are roasted in their own fat or simply thrown into the embers of the fireplace for five minutes. Once this cooking is done, they are presented on an upside down gazelle skin and each one is served without a fork.

This kind of experience makes you forget the mundane life. I found new joys, unknown emotions. I would stay in the tent and try to renew this wilderness as often as possible. The Bedouins seemed to love me, perhaps they loved me, because they felt that I understood their tastes and participated wholeheartedly in their joys. I jabbered a bit in Arabic, enough to put me in confidence with them.

One day when I had gone to the ruins of Resafa, lost in the desert, with two friends and a colonel, a man of letters, who was in command in Palmyra, we talked about the pilgrimage to Mecca, which Muslims from all over the world were preparing to make. One of the friends, whose husband was a sailor and was cruising in the Red Sea, told me how a sailor from the shore, going down to Djeddah make provisions, had been so seized by the silence of the city, the terror that seemed to reign there, the appearance of the inhabitants who brushed against the walls, the austerity maintained by the almighty police force of Ibn Saud, that he came back on board by snapping his teeth.

My curiosity was aroused and redoubled when, back in Palmyra, my cook told me that his sister had left for Mecca with a dozen Palmyreans.

These two impressions crystallized the vague, previously imprecise trends that my recent Bedouin experiences had given rise to.

I immediately offered to go with him to join these pilgrims, but this boy could not even tell me whether the group was traveling by land or by sea, and this stupidity made me fear to bring such a guide. But I did not give up my idea for that. By chance, Sattam came to see me in the afternoon with his suite in which was a certain Soleiman, Nedjien, who had served with the Palmyra Mehrarists. I had often met him in the Bedouin tent and had sometimes thought of taking him as a guide for a trip to the Nedj, but various chiefs had advised me against it. One cannot listen to everyone, and as I walked Sattam to the door I put my hand on Soleiman's shoulder and said to him : Stay, I have to talk to you.

We are then face to face and I ask :

– Do you still want to return to your tribe of Oneiza

He answers peacefully :

– For ten years now, I've had a daily desire to see my tribe again, but I lack the money to go so far.

I continue, seeing a favorable outcome to this conversation :

– Listen, I would like to travel all over Arabia and see your country, would you like to come with me ? Will you take me to your family, what relatives do you still have there ?

– My father and mother are in Oneiza with two of my sisters and a little brother. I have another sister married with a pearl fisherman in the Bahrain Islands in the Persian Gulf.

– Well, we will go pearl fishing.

– King Ibn Saud will never let you enter the Nedj.

– You will say that I am of your family; veiled, dressed as an Arab woman, I will look like a Bedouin.

– Yes, but if they find out the truth, they will cut your neck and cut mine off too.

– Well, I will marry you. Nothing can be blamed on you anymore, everything will be correct and legal.

This direct and new proposal surprises and interlocks Soleiman.

But he's getting his act together. As a Arab man that nothing surprises. He retorts quietly :

– What will your husband say ?

– What do you want him to say ? He won't object. I will not marry you as a male. I will not be yours. You will be my passport to make the trip. I will pay for everything for both of us and, on the return trip, as a baksheesh, I will give you double what we spent.

Soleiman meditates. He guesses for him a golden affair. His distrustful air abandons him. He is neither surprised nor outraged to serve me as a living identity card. I explain my project looking for the guarantees that could be useful to me :

– You understand that I want to come back alive. So you will have to contribute to the costs until I return, where everything will be reimbursed to you at double the amount... It must be in your interest to bring me back alive, because I know what I am risking.

He goes to consult his brothers and asks me for a few days of reflection.

– I give you two days.

I rush over to my husband's house to tell him about my new idea. He does not, in principle, condemn my project. He only had a bad premonition the next day. At night, sad dreams had haunted him, showing him the worst misfortunes for this trip. My decision is made, nothing can hold me back.

Twenty-four hours later, here is Soleiman.

He agreed and now only speaks to settle the details of the trip. Before Ahmed and Ali, my faithful servants, I make him swear protection and respect. He speaks a different Arabic than mine, so that Ahmed and Ali are necessary not to make any mistake or oddity in everything he calculates, plans and explains to me calmly.

In front of my brave and attentive servants, Soleiman promises, in an imaginative language, to avoid any fatigue and to ensure my comfort. This mission will be more precious to him than his life itself.

In order to seal the contract, he repeats three times, kissing his eyes : "This marriage will only be a sham for the government, Soleiman will respect you as his own sister".

This oath commits his honor and he will keep it. In fact, he kept it.

The deal was quickly concluded. But, before going any further, I need to give some details about the situation I had been in for some time. The dotal regime, under which I had been married to Pierre d'Andurain, constituted for us a heavy obstacle. I had been well tied up. So I was forced to look for a way to cancel this regime that had left me penniless. There was only one remedy : divorce.

We talked about it for a long time. It was a party that, necessarily, must have seemed strange and aroused enmity. But we resolved to do it and divorced with the understanding that we would be delighted. Pierre d'Andurain remained my true husband and continued to be my best friend. But, from a civil point of view, I was free.

FIRST OBSTACLES

WE HAD DECIDED TO LEAVE THE NEXT DAY, at dawn. No preparations, I'll leave as if I was going for a walk. No trunks. I will buy my Arabic costumes on the way... It is to forget, and with what joy, one of the miseries of all journeys.

Ali offers me as a gift a necklace of silver tubes containing suras from the Koran. It is a talisman.

Soon afterwards, I was to experience all the obstacles to my project from the odious administrative, governmental and political powers.

That same evening, as I was conversing with Pierre d'Andurain, Soleiman was announced. But I did not want to see him until the next day at the time of departure. He insisted and then explained to me that the colonel had just had his house searched.

The archaeological service of Beirut had, he said, filed a complaint against the poor boy for concealment of weapons and antiques. And he had to stand at the disposal of justice, in this case the colonel, to whom the complaint would have been transferred by the moudir.

I can guess a plot by the little colonel to prevent me from leaving, because I had been foolish enough to entrust my projects to him. I had done it, moreover, to tranquilize Soleiman who feared the military. So I asked my husband to accompany me to the colonel's house. This step annoyed him a lot, but he gave in to my desire. We leave. In spite of the late hour, with a smile on his lips and in his pyjamas, the little man of letters welcomes us with pleasure. He is fine and diplomatic. We drink champagne at his place. And I immediately attack my subject.

– Why, I say, this ridiculous measure against Soleiman ? You know very well that this complaint of the directorate of antiquities is unfounded.

He claims that he has the letter of complaint and that he must follow up on it.

I insist :

– The complaint is from the head of department ? From Seyrig ?

– Certainly.

I triumph without modesty

– As it so happens, Colonel, the director of the antique department is precisely in Palmyra, I would like to ask him to come and see you urgently, everything will be arranged.

The colonel does not flinch

– Certainly, madam, I will be delighted to see him.

I get up and walk to the door. But the colonel whispers in my husband's ear, and when we go out, Pierre confirms what I think :

– Naturally, he asked me not to send him the Director of

Antiquities. The complaint is a joke; what he wants is simply to see you give up your trip.

But it would take something else to change my decisions. I made an appointment with Soleiman for the next day. It will have to be on the square of the old village of Palmyra. And to all those I meet, or see, I say that I'm leaving for France. In the early morning, all my Arab friends come to greet me. Except for Ahmed and Ali, nobody suspects my true destination. They wish me a good trip, the car starts and heads towards the village where Soleiman is waiting for me walking on the square so as not to be noticed.

I'm a little anxious about this abduction right under the colonel's nose and I'm right, because the moment I arrive on the square a police car gets in the way of mine. We stop.

The brigadier comes down and asks me :

– Where are you going ?

I answer, furious

– It's none of your business.

But my Arab driver, unfortunately, is overzealous. He already said :

– We are going to Damascus.

The brigadier offers to escort me to Aïn Beïda, the first well on the road from Palmyra to Damascus.

I answer without kindness

– I don't need you. I have traveled this road a hundred times alone. Why do I need you to accompany me today ?

– I want to protect you, there have been reports of rezzous in the area.

– I'm not afraid of rezzous.

– I'm afraid for you.

– I am the only one to judge.

Seeing the dispute drag on and feeling that orders are being given, I understand that another ploy must be found. Because, if I had to declare war on the whole garrison of Palmyra, I will leave...

A new plan is forming in my mind. This time I will have the active help of my husband. He is irritated by Colonel Cottard's autocratic procedures. He fired his rifle, supposedly to hunt with Soleiman. He will thus bring him to the Palmyra pass, on the road to Damascus, where I will find him. And I wait nervously in the hotel lobby, surrounded by Arab friends and neighbors.

Suddenly, a car noise in front of the door. I lean out of the window and catch a glimpse of the colonel's eight-cylinder with himself getting out.

I save myself by giving the order to say I'm out. Ibrahim, a valet, joined me after a while. The big chief absolutely wants to see me. He asks me to come to his house, but he is very naive...

I watch outside and I see two machine gun cars coming back to Palmyra. It is still against me, they deploy all the offensive forces... I snub them and seeing the track of Damascus free, I get into the car.

An Arab, traveling to Damascus, accompanies me. He serves as justification. Nervously, I beg the driver to accelerate. A last glance at Palmyra. The car follows the valley of the Tombs. On the road, Pierre walks as usual. I take him in the car and he confides in my ear that Soleiman is hidden in a funeral tower.

At the designated place, my husband comes down and kisses me, then Soleiman appears and, in the most natural way in the world, asks me if I have room for him in the car. My husband, with a careless look, asks me to take him along.

– Yes, get in quickly !

The comedy succeed.

We're driving fast, I'm exulting and thinking about the future. I try to guess the unknown and violent emotions of the perils to be run.

Soleiman, on the other hand, seems worried. He has not yet weighed the possible consequences of this equation. He fears reprisals from King Ibn Saud, if the deception is discovered. I give him a Kalinin pill to numb his apparent anxiety. I try to cheer him up. Then I question the other Arab in French. Soleiman does not understand my language. The Arab, who knows it, confides to me that my future husband has a bad reputation as a proud, proud, ambitious man. But he is a warrior and he has that rare sense of the desert that made him used by the French officers. We arrive in Damascus at night. Soleiman does not hide his admiration for the meadows, waterfalls and olive groves that surround this pearl of the East.

I enter the hotel, he has to come to take my orders tomorrow at eight o'clock.

Naturally, we must organize the steps prior to the celebration of our wedding. I only have one month to do so, I left Palmyra on the morning of March 9 and it is on April 9 that the ceremonies of El Arafat begin, the beginning of the prayers that are indispensable for the moral validity of any pilgrimage.

A Muslim who did not attend these demonstrations would no longer be entitled to the special graces of the peeler. A believer, even if he has spent a year in Madinah or Mecca, has the title of "Hajj" only if he has performed this sacred rite. Tradition says that it was on this hill that Adam and Eve, driven from the earthly paradise, separated, having even wandered for years in search of each other, finally met. Hence the name of the mountain, El Arafat, which means : the mountain of recognition.

The next day, Soleiman comes one hour late to the promised appointment. But, reassured, he smiles blissfully. He is accompanied by an Arab whom he says is secretary at the Nedj consulate.

Soleiman immediately applies for a baksheesh for this Nedjien, in order, he says, to facilitate things with the consul. I categorically refuse. He has to lose this annoying habit of considering me as an open bank.

We leave through the city, towards the consulate. There reigns an absolutely new atmosphere, one feels in the most delicate tradition of true Islam. A menzul consecrates the importance of the house; it is a room where coffee is served permanently to all visitors. Let us imagine the charcoal fire of bots, in the middle of the room, on which several long spout coffeemakers are constantly heating up. Servants serve coffee and offer cigarettes.

We don't drink, we want to see the consul.

It is Sheik Abdel Raouf.

Here he is right on the stairs : a dignified, almost majestic man. His costume is simple, but the kéfié is restrained by a golden agal, a sign of his important function. With a solemn gesture, he asks us to follow him to his office.

He sits down without a word, with his hand pointing to seats and in a deaf voice he asks the interpreter to question us.

As I would like to lead the conversation, I take the floor :

– Can a French woman obtain a passport for Djeddah ?

If he is astonished, the sheik does not let it be seen. Not a muscle in his face moves. He stares at me alone, with a straight and deep sharpness, then the interpreter gives me his answer :

What do you want to do in Djeddah ?

I want to travel and penetrate the heart of Islam. I have lived a lot with the Arabs, who constantly visit holy places and the forbidden Nedj. I am attracted to the religion of Allah and I want to convert to Islam.

He does not comment on my words, but retorts in an equal tone :

– I cannot give you a passport for Djeddah, but that itself would not help you, since you need the king's permission to enter the interior.

– Fine, but if you don't want to give me a passport, will you marry me to Soleiman ?

– If you really intend to marry him, why didn't you marry in Palmyra ?

– It was impossible, I'm too well known and they would have put an obstacle in the way.

– Do you really love Soleiman ?

On my affirmative answer, Soleiman swaggered and strutted. The consul remains frozen, but his questions show a growing mistrust.

– Will you become a Muslim only to marry Soleiman ?

– No way. Even if I couldn't marry him, I would convert. So marry us here without any fear. I want to avoid complications with my government, because they will not look favorably on a French woman becoming a Nedjian and a Muslim.

Abdel Raouf asks me if I can have as witnesses two members of the High Commissioner's Office.

– I have just told you that I want to keep my project secret until its completion.

– Well, continues the consul, you just have to come back tomorrow. I'll find out and I'll tell you yes or no.

– Why wait ? It is useless to waste time, you know that. It's so much easier to get married right away.

– Tomorrow.

– If you're determined to say no, say it now. I will leave informed.

– Tomorrow, come back, I'll do my best, said Sheikh Abdel

Raouf.

I return to the hotel almost satisfied. This interview, in truth, leaves me hopeful. Served, as has often happened to me, by chance, I then meet the Secretary of the President of the Syrian Republic, with one of my friends, a French adviser to the Public Works, Here are my two witnesses this time, both very official officials, one from the French government, the other from the Syrian government. It is true that we need their signatures. I invite them to lunch. I explain my intentions and, after a minute of amazement, they agree to do me this service. The next day, as soon as I am in the presence of the consul, I tell him that I have official witnesses.

– This cannot be enough. I want Mr. Véber, the French delegate in Damascus.

Furious, I protest :

– It's a mockery, you've been asking around since our interview yesterday and you've certainly been told that I'm in a deadly scramble with this official. It is impossible for me to involve him.

The consul answers laconically :

– I can only unite you in the presence of Mr. Véber; if you don't want to, go get married elsewhere.

This is a terrible complication. There is a Nedj consul only here, in Cairo and London. This is probably the place where Abdel Raouf sends me. The consul has now refused. He explains to me that I will only have a chance of success in Egypt or Palestine, because these two countries are not under French mandate. He does not want to risk trouble with the authorities by marrying a French woman to a Nedjian.

There upon the meeting was adjourned. I am disappointed, dissatisfied and concerned.

What am I going to do ?

In any case, I will first of all leave Damascus. I am first leaving with Soleiman for Beirut where I want to bid farewell to my youngest son, a student at the American University. He disapproves of my plan to travel to the Persian Gulf. Not that the idea, in itself, seems bad to him. Above all, he would like me to take the time to perfect my Arabic, which will betray me immediately. In addition, he tells me that it would take a year of Muslim studies to be ready to carry out exactly the rites of the pilgrimage.

I obviously do not accept this advice. I want to make the trip this year. Next year, who knows if I'll still want to ?

Almost everyone ignores my project. Those who do know it, however, are rather gloomy; some predict my death, others life imprisonment, at least several years in a harem in Oneiza.

Nothing distracts me, the risks I am told about are only new attractions. We leave for Haifa. It is the first city in Palestine and I hope to be able to marry my indispensable Soleiman there. We reach Saida, a small port crouching in the sand in the sun. A white street streaked with purple shadows. Africans, Arabs, women in a dazzling harmony. Bunches of children offer us giant tangerines with outstretched arms. Dust and sunshine, we are still driving.

Nakura, border. Disheveled customs officers play belote, spit, smoke pipes. I gave a lesson to Soleiman. He must pretend not to know me. His Nedjien passport allows him to pass without difficulty from one country to another.

Luckily, mine is also stamped without complications. The road is cornice on piles of red, yellow and pink rocks, dug with soft and powerful shadows. At the English customs, cut steeply, the mountain overlooks the sea. On its side, the road is laid out like a balcony. Soleiman, who has never left the desert, admires, meditates and seems to have difficulty understanding reality.

We finally arrive on the sand of Haifa beach. The waves come to die under the tires of the car and erase as its tracks are made.

CONVERSION

IN HAIFA AND IN SPITE OF THE TEMPTATION of its houses buried in the greenery on the mountainside, I want an Arabic hotel. Soleiman, hurried to this effect, chooses, without vain meditations, the first one that presents itself.

A room with two beds... I share the room with my future husband. Of course, I am prepared for this event, but finally a certain anxiety comes to me. Will Soleiman keep his promise ? Without warning me, he has already informed the manager Azem about the adventure that brings us both together. Azem is honest, considerate, complacent and very disinterested. He has been placed on our road by a favorable destiny and here he is, running to find dear Sheikh Tewfik, who, according to him, can perfectly marry us. Soleiman strolls in the room. He smiles when he meets a mirror and spits on the floor with dignity. He has a kind of humiliating alopecia, which he carefully hides under his kefié. I didn't realize it until I saw him rubbing his head. He would like to use one of my bottles for this purpose. Naturally, I refuse. But I realize that he has already opened my suitcase and taken some hair lotion, only it's for the hands... I try in vain to convince him that it's not a perfume and that it smells bad.

The sheik arrives. He is a venerable old man with a white goatee. His dress is fine beige serge, closed from top to bottom by a series of small matching buttons. A coat of the same fabric with wide flared sleeves opens at the front and floats at the back. His white pleated turban is mounted in a crown on the dark red tarbouche. Its silhouette is slim and elegant. We receive him in our room. Soleiman and I are each sitting on our bed and he sits on a chair between us. Azem attends the interview. The sheik begins with a short Islamic catechism speech for me.

He insists on the four main points of his religion :

– You will be pure, not only through the five usual ablutions, the five prayers of day and night, but also through your heart, your feelings, your thoughts, your desires. Outward purity consists in avoiding everything that could pollute you. It involves nails cut short, total hair removal, a shaved beard, combed hair, and even, what didn't matter to me, circumcision. Tradition claims that Muhammad was born circumcised.

The five daily prayers are called :

Soba (dawn); Dohor (noon); Aser (afternoon); Maghreb (sunset); Icha (night)

The sheik then whispers the classic prayer, which I transcribe in my road book :

"I certify that only God is God and that Muhammad is his prophet."

– You will say this prayer, said the sheik, before dawn, at noon, as soon as the sun begins to go down, at sunset, and at nightfall.

You will precede each of these prayers with an ablution. A man shall not take a full bath until he has lived with a woman or has approached a dead body, and you, woman, shall suppress your prayers after your diapers and at the time of your periods. Then you would be too impure to invoke the name of Allah.

In the cities, the times of prayers will be indicated to you by the muezzin from the top of the minarets. You will not go to the mosque, but you will make your acts of faith in the harem (Muslims believe that the presence of women in mosques with them could put them in a state of sin by suggesting to them ideas other than those they should have in the house of Allah).

I interrupt the sheik to ask him :

– How will I make an ablution, without water, in the desert ?

– You will take fine sand or dust in your hand and rub your body according to the usual ritual.

The sheik then moves on to the second point

– You will give alms.

Alms consists of voluntary alms giving and legal alms, i.e. instituted by religion. They consist in giving a day of one's fortune in money, camels, sheep, dates, cereals, etc., to the people. The divine precepts command to give a fifth of the profits made from trade and business.

The third point deals with fasting. (Here again, the religion of the prophet does not place itself solely from the point of view of food but gives this abstention a hygienic character).

– You will refrain from any thought that might lead you away from God. During Ramadan, you shall not eat, drink, or consent to the acts of the flesh from sunrise to sunset. You will recognize the dawn when you can distinguish a white thread from a black thread. If you have your periods, you are unclean and must eat, just as if you are sick. But you will fast at the end of the four hundred days, the exact number of days you have missed.

To convince me, the Sheikh quotes, with all due dignity, this phrase from the Prophet :

"The smell of the mouth of the fasting person is more pleasing to God than the smell of musk".

For the fourth point, the Sheikh reminds me that every good Muslim should make the pilgrimage to Mecca at least once before dying, repeating with the Prophet :

"It would be better to die a Christian or a Jew than to die a Muslim without having been to Mecca".

One understands the full scope of this sentence when one thinks that the worst insult is to call someone a Christian or a Jew.

One cannot but admire the strength of a faith that moves thousands of people every year from all parts of the world, to bring them all together in the same holy place, which is particularly difficult to access. It is also an expense that requires most pilgrims years of savings and deprivation.

The sheik ends his teaching by summarizing it by this maxim of the khalife Omar-Ebn-Abdel-Aziz :

"Prayer leads us halfway to the throne of God, fasting puts us at the door of his palace and charity gives us entrance".

The muezzin's complaint suddenly resounded, calling out to the faithful in his sad and guttural voice.

We bow down and prostrate with all our foreheads on the ground. My first prayer is to Allah.

From today I am forbidden to sin, eat pork, drink wine and alcohol, play cards or any other game of chance for money. Usury is of course forbidden and even the charging of normal interest : money deposited in the bank must not yield any interest.

I still fulfill the formalities that Sheikh Tewfik asks for : I indicate the date of my birth, the name of my father, my mother, etc. The Sheikh then goes to the cadi to ask for the authorization to celebrate our marriage and my conversion.

Soleiman and I are looking forward to seeing our business take such a good turn. I go to bed fully dressed and watch Soleiman from the corner of my eye. I see him coming back from his ablutions, he takes off his coat and his brown dress, keeping only his large white tennoura as a shirt. We politely wish each other a good night and he covers his kéfié's head, folding all the blankets over his face : a desert habit to protect his face.

The next day, I wake Soleiman up early so that he can go and find out the result of the steps taken with the cadi. Azem, seeing him somnolent, proposes to replace him in this mission, because he knows the city and especially the way to proceed in such a case.

He comes back at nine o'clock with a radiant face. Sheikh Tewfik is indeed waiting for us at the end of the morning. We go there. There are present all the notables necessary for the public celebration of my conversion. The women receive me in their apartments, telling me that everyone is deliberating with seriousness about the religious problems posed by such a delicate case.

The sheik's wife, ugly and dirty, quietly washes her kitchen. She is a good housekeeper, but her daughter, young and outrageously made-up, is in a hurry to make the hat and veil that I will wear once I am converted. We understand each other as best we can. After a while a question burns their tongues: they want to know if it is true that I gave two thousand pounds of gold to Soleiman.

For the young man doesn't waste a minute to take care of his publicity and he displays imaginary wealth. Moreover, my reputation of opulence does not fail to help us, by giving rise everywhere to an obsessive kindness.

The sheik calls me. The great religious council has finished its deliberations, he says, and he comes to me with majesty, to make me understand the importance of the act I am about to perform. I immediately cover myself with the obligatory black veil. I introduce myself to the assembly. The minute is quite imposing. It's not just the decor that contributes to it : a bourgeois salon with polychrome velvet armchairs. The notables are lined up along the wall. There is the sheik, the paskaté (first after the cadi), a secretary, three witnesses, and a lawyer interpreter.

I listen, standing, to the sheik who speaks to me, while the others approve by nodding their heads.

– Woman, do you only make yourself a Muslim to marry Soleiman ? By the Prophet, answer.

– Why would I convert, if only to marry Soleiman ? A Muslim can marry a woman of another religion. If I prostrate myself before Allah, it is because I believe in his omnipotence.

The consistory rises and forms a circle around me. The lawyer, a young man dressed in European style and wearing a tarbouche, detaches himself from the group and moves forward, asking me to repeat after him, in French and Arabic, word for word : "Echadou Allah, Illallah, etc."

"I swear that there is only one God, that God alone is God, that Muhammad is God's messenger. I believe in his apostles, in his books and in the last day.

No blasphemy against the religion of my ancestors. On the contrary, a striking similarity with our Creed.

I swore. The ceremony is almost over, however I still have to change my marital status. I have to choose an Arabic name, I decide for that of Zeinab, one of the favorite women of the Prophet and also that of the former queen of Palmyra, Zenobia. Then follows the administrative part, that is to say the signature of the witnesses, the paskaté, the sheik and Soleiman, not knowing how to write, replace his signature by the print of his thumb, inked on a stamp plate. My new personality signs in French and Arabic "Zeînab".

I am a little worried about this new name, this second "me" that will now have to hide all the reactions, all the thoughts, all the words that could prevent me from succeeding in the expedition that I have undertaken.

My official conversion is recorded, it was simple, like all the important ceremonies of the Arabs, without pomp. In reality, this lack of pomp gives a more solemn character to the act itself, concentrating all thoughts on the moral significance of the ceremony.

Is there not more eloquence in this simplification than in our Western rites ? On the other hand, the legal formalities are not yet finished. The governor of Haifa must sign the agreement and make it valid or null and void with these simple words :

The term "favourable" or "unfavourable".

The days are now spent waiting for this signature. I begged Sheikh Tewfik to marry us, without wasting any time, but he refers to the cadi who does not dare to take any decision without the authorization of the great muphti of Jerusalem, currently the greatest religious leader of all Islam, since the suppression of the one of Constantinople.

One cannot blame the precautions of the cadi, however exasperating they may be. The case is very special. Indeed, we are foreigners, without residence in Palestine and I am a new convert. I must see the governor and obtain his signature, without which my conversion is null. For three days, pain lost, he is never there, or he is busy. I insist so much by going back there in the morning, afternoon and evening that he finally receives me.

Fortunately, he is a Muslim, therefore in principle favorable to my conversion; however, he insists in vain on the illegality of this act, which should have been carried out in the real place of my residence.

He is a gentleman, courteous, gallant. Finally, he signs : "Favourable opinion".

The first set is won. It still remains to obtain the final act which must emanate from Jerusalem in three or four days.

The faithful Azem accompanies me everywhere. Soleiman, always dodges himself to sleep, drink coffee, smoke, in order to forget his nostalgia of the desert. This city atmosphere suffocates him. He repeats incessantly : "Ah ! Zeînab, where are the tents, the great silence of the day and especially of the night, the rhythm of the pestle in the mortar ?"

I spend the days walking alone along the sea, or I buy some provisions : bread, olives, cottage cheese, meatballs, which I eat in my room. A Muslim woman should not go to a restaurant. One day, in a street, I see a fortune teller crouching on the sidewalk in front of a small handkerchief covered with sand. More than ever, I want to know what the future holds for me. I crouch on the ground and, in the middle of the group, exhilarated by the freedom and incognito that my veil gives me, I mark with my finger dots on the sand, corresponding to the number of letters of the word "Zeînab". In a low voice, the oracle confides to me :

– You'll have a great trip, but you'll also have great troubles and great disputes with the Government.

Without believing it for a moment, I am however satisfied, the main thing is the success, I will always triumph over the difficulties.

I usually find Soleiman, in the evening, in our room, smoking his hookah and spitting on the tile floor. We talk from one bed to the other and I get to know the dominant traits of his character : pride, boasting, laziness, greed. It appears that he will be able to enjoy all my fortune, which he supposes to be immense. He likes to talk about money, to evaluate the situation that he will have in Palmyra at the time of his return. I can repeat to him that I will keep strictly the contract that was signed at the time of the departure, but he has the audacity to tell me one evening :

– You'll buy me a Buick, won't you ? as soon as we get back to Syria and then we'll go to France. Who will we live with in Paris ?

– I will go down to my brother's house, who has a much more violent character than me.

Soleiman is afraid and mutters that he will go to the hotel.

He explains to me that he is a virgin and that one of his greatest desires is to have many children. I promise to buy him women at the Nedj.

– Not right away when we arrived, he said, because of my family and King Ibn Saud, who would have our heads cut if he suspected that we were not really married.

One morning, on his way back from his ablutions, he wipes his face with my towel; I strongly enjoin him to be careful not to use my personal belongings. Soleiman seems very upset, he is convinced that one can only admire him. In addition, he remains convinced, in spite of all my rebuffs, that I have a little feeling for him. Soleiman complains at every moment that I tire him and break his head. Of course, I push him around a little, but he is so inert that he exasperates me.

Walking through the streets, I meet the lawyer that served as my interpreter for my conversion. He insists that I go to his house for coffee. I accept against all Muslim rules. A few days later, I receive a letter written like a page from a child's school calligraphy notebook, the letters are one centimeter high and still say : "Madam, you are so rich and intelligent, why don't you marry a cultured man like me ? You can judge by the little Anglo-Arab textbook that I created in the Palestinian police station and that I gave to you a few days ago. Why marry this ignorant Soleiman who will never be able to understand you ?"

It is a direct marriage proposal. My lawyer is after my fortune and makes no secret of it.

As everything keeps hanging around, I decide to spend the weekend in Beirut, to see my young son again. I entrust Soleiman with our interests in Haifa while I'm away, and of course I leave with a veil on.

On my return, I find Soleiman more amorphous than ever, and without any news of the formalities in progress. I call the Grand Mufti in Jerusalem, he promises me an answer within forty-eight hours. After this lapse of time, the Paskaté, whom I disturb twice a day, finally tells me that the Grand Mufti authorized the Cadi to marry us, as soon as I would have the official deed confirming my conversion.

So many complications ! So governments are all the same ? The last obstacle that I'm facing is not legal, but my situation is too delicate for me to try to protest.

Things continue to drag on so much that I suddenly decide to leave for Jerusalem to try something else. It is a question of getting the visa for our passports from the Egyptian Consulate. Then we will try to take the boat in Suez and this by writing ourselves, in Arabic, on Soleiman's passport :

"Zeinab, bent Mohamed".

"Zeinab, Mohamed's daughter".

Arab women do not appear in front of the Consuls and don't give out photos or any other piece of identity, this must succeed. Desert Bedouins have no marriage certificate. Why not give it a try ?

Hasn't Soleiman, faced with the incessant procedures we've been taking over the last two weeks, told me a hundred times : "Bedouins never make a marriage certificate; when we agree on the price of a woman, it's over".

So let him present himself to the Consulate and the Navigation Company as a Bedouin with his Bedouin wife, without a contract, and that's it.

I also want to find out about the departure dates of the boats for Djeddah, a line that is not very busy outside the special services of the pilgrimage. The slowness and prevarication of Soleiman, who is always short of cigarettes and coffee at the local kawagi, delays our departure, so much that we arrive in Jerusalem to attend the closing of the Consulate of Egypt. I walk through the door of the first hotel that comes and do not hide my displeasure from him, from which he cowardly escapes by slipping away.

He comes back in the afternoon, embarrassed, and responds with dignity to my request for an explanation of his conduct :

– Madam, didn't you see that everyone in this hotel is Jewish ?

– Idiot, how do you know that the people in this hotel are Jewish ? You don't know them any better than I do.

– Allah be praised, be pleased, Madam, he said, it is all arranged, we will have the passports in three days, the company sent mine to Cairo, to the Nedjian Consulate, to have your name added to it as my wife. The shipping company has sold its tickets for the pilgrimage like any other Nedjian couple.

The solution seems good to me, but I'm still worried that he may have been tricked by this travel agency, which naturally wanted to provide him with two passages. In any case, he acted with total unconsciousness, depriving himself of his passport.

We return the next day to Haifa. A very pleasant trip in the evening light. Soleiman doesn't say a word, dozing in a corner like a groundhog.

When I pay the driver, with whom I had agreed a price of three

Palestinian pounds, Soleiman says to me with a haughty air :

– Give him a pound of tip.

Regardless of his arrogance and his tone of command, I slip into the driver's hand a few piasters, tip in proportion to the total sum. The driver, having heard Soleiman, follows us down the stairs. Soleiman, with emphasis, gives the order to the hotelier to pay this sum. I turn around angrily, forbidding the owner to do so because I am in charge. But the latter, encouraged by Soleiman's gestures and winks, after some hesitation, secretly hands the money to the driver, thinking that I wouldn't notice him. I saw the gesture, exploded, I got angry as never before we have seen a Muslim woman get angry, and told the hotel owner :

– You will not be paid and I leave the hotel right away, while, turning back to Soleiman, I shout to him :

– You're just a poser and an idiot.

Humiliated by these public insults, he climbs up the stairs like a big star, draping himself in his coat and saying :

– Ana Emir. (I am an emir.)

I burst out laughing, shrugging my shoulders, while the Arabs, witnesses of this scene, look at him with a mixture of respect, admiration and astonishment.

WEDDING

HOWEVER I AM TIRED OF THESE SCENES OF household, stupidity, fatuity of my partner and I leave as I announced.

I wander for a long time on the beach, then I walk on a long road lined with cemeteries, especially the English army, so calm in its greenery and flowers, so restful in its perfect order. For hours I have been walking, dreaming and hesitating for the first time to go with this man. He exasperates me so much that I wonder how I will be able to bear his stupidity and gaffes any longer.

I am seriously thinking of going back to Palmyra, when I see two silhouettes, one in dress and kéfié, the other in pants and tarbouche, which come to my meeting are Soleiman and Azem who have been looking for me, it seems, for a long time; my "passport husband" did not dare to come to me, alone. He counts on the sympathy I have for Azem, and uses it as a buffer. But I am deaf to their kindness and keep a stubborn silence. I finally break it only to refuse Soleiman to go to the cinema with him in the evening, a colossal and ultimate offer with which he hoped to soften me, since all his requests for forgiveness had not touched me.

They begged me to stay, promised to carry out all my desires from now on. Soleiman did not realize the value of money. He had been mistaken several times, considering that the piaster was worth one-fifth of the franc, as in Syria, whereas in Palestine, the piaster is the unit. I had not been able to make him understand this until now, but I took advantage of his distress to settle the pecuniary question between us. I notified him that I would no longer entrust him with a penny. During my two-day absence in Beirut, had he not spent several pounds, without being able to explain to me how they were used ?

The day after this scene, we go to the "makamé charayé", a religious court, where we finally found out that my certificate has arrived. I am a Muslim in good and due form, as attested by the justification document in Arabic and English. The Cadi authorizes the marriage and, in a short and eloquent speech, wishes us joy and prosperity. He envies our happiness to be able to go to Mecca.

We send Azem in search of Sheikh Tewfik, with the very precious paper, while we return to the hotel to prepare the wedding ceremony and departure.

First of all, I have to find witnesses; I talk to everyone I can find : the hotel owner, his brother, and then passers-by in the street, among them two porters in big blue sweaters, on which "Hotel Khédivial" is written in huge white letters. They seem bewildered by my proposal, but they accept it, as much to receive the baksheesh that I offer them, as for the prospect of attending wedding celebrations. We are obligious to close the doors to all the kind passers-by who are now offering their services.

We use as mosque the central corridor, on which all the rooms look out, because the hotel does not have a lounge. It is a kind of corridor rather wide, at the top of a staircase. We have a row of armchairs for assistance.

Azem still has not appeared again, he runs in search of Sheik Tewfik; it is all the more ridiculous that we met this charac-ter on our return and that he is here now. But it is an event that seems incredible. Everybody is shouting, screaming. The sheik, moreover, refuses to marry us without having   the act of autorization which is in Azem's hands. He is wary of this haste, which may well be hiding a trap, and which is really just a complicated arrangement scenario.

Some assistants ask for the sweets that are traditional in such circumstances. I didn't know this and I make up for it by distributing money to the witnesses, who go out in a general stampede for expensive customary sweets. The first brings back dairy products, half curdled milk, half starch, covered with a pistachio hash decoration. Next come round, white cakes, a kind of very dry meringues, which fall into powder at the first bite. Candied fruits, sugar syrups, roses, almond honey cakes complete this delight.

I am sitting next to Soleiman who is not much more moved than I am. The marriage begins with the estimation of my market value. The price is set at one thousand Turkish pounds gold. It is always my reputation of wealth that has gotten me into the worst trouble. I recuse myself and drop the price by offering the hundredth, ten pounds.

Consternation in the assembly. We go to 500. I counter-propose 25, then 50, finally we agree on the price of one hundred pounds.

So I buy myself a hundred pounds of gold, to call myself Mrs. Abdel-Aziz Deckmari. My marriage certificate will mention that Soleiman paid me one hundred pounds.

After the auction, the ceremony continues; Soleiman gets up with a yawn and disappears without a word of explanation; a sudden burst of discretion gave his untimely absence an explanation that I found plausible, but the audience attributed it to a natural need.

Five minutes, Soleiman doesn't come back...

Ten minutes, Soleiman didn't come back...

A quarter of an hour later, Soleiman is still not there...

The sheik, speaking to me, explains that the custom of marriage consecrates a donation to the mosque. of Omar. I call Soleiman. No answer, general desolation. Azem, who still carries the famous authorization, was sent to look for the sheik, who is right here, but he has not yet returned either.

The complications of this comedy annoy me more and more.

After twenty minutes, Soleiman returns alone, unhurriedly with his eternal smile; he explains that he went to the hairdresser to have his beauty treated. It's all about being beautiful and getting a shave when everyone is in the middle of the ceremony.

I insist that we stop procrastinating. The formalities are resuming at the point where they had been interrupted. Sheikh Tewfik hands us a receipt with a white background and a mosque printed in yellow, the receipt is an honorary distinction and a blessing at the same time. We sign the final deed, all that remains is to leave.

The congratulations and hints of our honeymoon begin. Soleiman is advised to kiss me. I dissuade him with a lightning glance that I accompany with a significant gesture, to which he responds with a clever look :

"She loses nothing to wait, I'll teach her the little game tonight..."

Boasting, I remain impassive, satisfied that he plays his difficult role of husband in public as well.

My irritation is at its height, everything is signed, finished : it is the decisive moment, but the sheik, as a good civil servant, wants to be covered and hold the famous authorization that runs after him, with Azem, our faithful secretary. Prayers, supplications, threats, finally make him give in... the marriage certificate is in my bag... I pull Soleiman sharply by the arm, we let our witnesses and our makeshift guests making wishes for our happiness. They seem dismayed at such a quick departure. We throw ourselves into the car with our luggages and leave Haifa at full speed by the road to Jerusalem. I am nervous and hectic in one corner, in the other Soleiman is composed the attitude of an emir, with all the dignity of the nobility he has attributed to himself.

My first words as a legitimate wife are to express my displeasure at the tasteless publicity he gave to our marriage. Indeed, I heard the same morning that in Palestine, the country's daily newspaper with highest circulation, had announced my marriage to a certain Soleiman, to whom I offered half a million.

– We have to hide, why spread out this marriage that must remain secret ? By Allah, you are foolish, yes, foolish and stubborn.

He apologizes, explaining to me that this marriage has made him lose his head, he had not understood. And, all the time of the trip, he repeats like a chorus :

– I am very lucky...

We arrive in Jerusalem, we rush through the bustling streets to the navy company. There is no passport, of course, the employees claim to have sent it to Suez where there is supposedly a Nedjian consular officer at the time of the pilgrimage. They ask us to wait three days. We have already missed the boat of March 18, the last one leaving Beirut, we also miss the boat of March 24, leaving Suez, which was the last connection with the pilgrimage. However, the company tells us that an Italian cargo ship will leave Suez on the 29th... " Inch Allah " (*God willing).*

My dominant desire remains Oneiza, then the crossing of Arabia on foot and in caravan, and to that I do not want to give up.

Mecca is not my main goal, but I would think it would be stupid to arrive there eight days after the religious rites of the pilgrimage. So I live in a proud expectation and, to shake a little the negligent impassibility of my "passport husband", I warn him that, if we do not embark on the 29th, I renounce my projets and I return to Palmyra.

To enter Mecca, all you have to do is be a good Muslim for two years, as the book says. So in two years I will be able to go there.

Soleiman has taken a liking to his new situation.

He throws himself on my knees, kisses my hands, begs me to be patient. Every day he goes to the company to hasten and activate the necessary steps. He will make phone calls to Cairo, to Suez. He is radiantly optimistic. He will succeed.

In the meantime, here I am, wandering through the abundance of holy places that is Jerusalem. I go from the Garden of Olives to the Wailing Wall, from the Mosque of Omar to the Holy Sepulcher. I come to forget my new religion and I enter veiled in this last sanctuary to kneel, in good catholic, in front of the three footprints edged with copper and left by the crosses of the Messiah Jesus and the two thieves.

Prostrated, I embrace the divine traces, when I get up to see the silhouette of a lady of a certain age who lives in the hotel where we are staying.

I had noticed her and felt that she was interested in me. Her stunned look made me understand the unfortunate nature of a situation I wasn't even thinking about. Zeinab's convictions had remained outside, but I had entered the Holy Sepulchre in her costume. I remained in prayer, embarrassed and feeling the gaze of this unknown friend weighing down on me. I wanted to avoid having a conversation with her, because it was impossible for me to explain facts that I did not want to reveal to anyone. So I remained immersed in my prayers.

But the lady, Mrs. Amoun, remained there, as patient as I was. After a long time, she put her hand on my shoulder and whispered :

– Don't be afraid, I won't betray you.

Her face exuded kindness and she understood my concern. Seeing the impossibility of escaping this commiseration, all made of sympathy, I got up and followed her in silence. Even before we left the Holy Sepulchre, she whispered to me in the darkness that was favorable to painful confidences :

– How did you marry this man ?

Strange way to start... But the brave person could not hold back her affection and her infinite curiosity. To answer anything other than the truth was impossible for me. But I could not tell the reality. I nodded melancholically.

The elderly and compassionate lady concludes :

– It is fatality.

I'm not sentimental, but her kindness and her visible anguish, inspired me confidence.

I accompanied her without saying anything. She first gave me the honors of the church. Then we went down into the underground passages and she was moved by the places where, according to tradition, some martyrs have been executed. We entered the most sacred place of all, the Holy Sepulchre.

I lifted my veil, according to Mrs. Amoun's wish. But life is full of paradoxical surprises. As soon as I am revealed, I find myself face to face with Syrian air force officers. I can't avoid them, for we are under the low white marble door at the entrance to Christ's tomb, and we have to follow the line. I tell them to give some of my news to my husband when they go to Palmyra. They are visibly very surprised, they imagined that I was going to France and they find me dressed as a Muslim in the holy places, followed by an old lady and a gentleman (her nephew) in tarbouche.

Mrs. Amoun offers me a walk and I follow her. She looks like one of my old provincial aunts and her nephew completes the bizarre picture we form. He is dressed in the European style, his tarbouche is the only oriental note.

This time, I frankly explain to Mrs. Amoun my situation with Soleiman, my desire to travel and my white marriage. She seems flabbergasted at the idea that I am sharing a room with an unknown Arab for the sole purpose of accomplishing a difficult journey.

She apologizes for her own astonishment and asks me :

– Aren't you afraid to sleep in the same room as this man ? He looks so mean, he's spawning me.

– Fear, but why ? The poor boy is nonchalant and proud, but without malice.

She persists in judging Soleiman a "terror".

I'm not arguing anymore. You don't change people's opinions.

PASSPORT

FROM THAT DAY ON, I TOOK ALL MY MEALS with Mrs. Amoun and her nephew in the hotel's Management Room. I gave up taking my meals, as before, in my room, so as not to attract attention. The curiosities wear out.

Soleiman used to take *"mezzés" (1)* in the dining room, but at another table. He did it before or after me, so as not to be humiliated. If I arrived before he left, he would smoke his hookah and look so ecstatic that he really seemed not to see me. In this case, Mrs. Amoun's nephew, Mr. Gabbour, teased him by treating him with an affected respect and telling him about his many affairs.

He joked about the frivolity of his "wife Zeinab". Soon after, we were vaccinated against smallpox, choera, typhus and the plague. It is de rigueur for all pilgrims. Mr. Gabbour then had the idea to ask, in front of Soleiman, to see the vaccinations I had been given above the knee, in order to push my Bedouin a little out of his hinges.

The joke was in pretty bad taste, but it entertained Mr. Gabbour so much that I agreed. We had dinner and then waved to Soleiman to come and have coffee with us.

(1) *Arabic hors d'oeuvre.*

66

Mr. Gabbour, with seriousness and compunction, begins to question him about the tribe he is emir of, his herds and his interests in the desert. Soleiman lied with ease and dignity. He spoke of the abundance of his immense herds, of the transactions of camels which he carried out by thousands, and his pride flourished widely. Mr. Gabbour made him speak without respite. Soleiman, exhilarated, takes great pleasure in inventing ever more mirific details. Finally, he is asked about the formalities to be completed to leave :

– It's all over, we were vaccinated today.

Mr. Gabbour slides down the slope offered.

– Zeinab too ?

I answer :

– Of course, here you go, this is the mark of my vaccines ! And, joining the gesture to the word, I raise my skirt above the knee…

This time Soleiman sees red. He gets up, out of his mind, and takes me by the arm. We go back to our room where he complains and reproaches in abundance. He can see that I often have fun at his costs. But something like that, in public, is beyond the measure. He perorates :

– Not only do you walk again on the streets, but you talk with men, with Christians, and you show a secret part of your body to these strangers. It's impossible to understand why I put up with this, our subterfuge is going to be discovered and you are putting us in great danger.

Then his usual refrain reappears :

– You don't love me at all, you make fun of me, you don't trust me.

Weary and annoyed, I explain to him :

– You bore me with your perpetual complaints. I'll tell you that everyone, seeing you as you are, advises me not to leave in your company. They think you're going to kill me in the desert. And yet, you see that I do not give up. If I didn't trust you, would I leave ? Because soon, in your country, we'll be alone and you can do whatever you want with me.

He is hit.

– Ma'am, you're right, I'm sorry.

All moved, he steps forward to put a kiss on my forehead. I push him away sharply and he moves away, melancholy.

Other scenes, moreover, are constantly renewed. I reproach him for this hookah that he smokes without respite, in our room, spitting and coughing constantly. I then open the windows, but he wants them closed.

– You want to kill me, he said. It's not the hookah that hurts me, it's the wind and cold that you let in.

Finally, he gives in and lies down, buried under his kéfié and a heap of blankets. But I was, it must be said, perpetually irritated by its unbearably softness. It took tenacity and activity to bring our project to fruition and we were constantly busy. But he was always drowsy. I had to shake him to remind him of an urgent step. He would reply immediately :

– Go yourself ! I'm so tired and you're so much more skillful !

These censer strokes did not take much, so much more so that in many circumstances I could not appear without risking leaving my role of Bedouin.

– Me, tired, a lot, me, he repeated.

And so our stay in Jerusalem extended beyond the limits of what we could have imagined. In such a way that we soon ran out of money. We had combined the financial side of our trip with great care. Pilgrims, we couldn't carry more than thirty pounds each, that's the law. But we had made checks for twenty-five pounds in the name of Soleiman at the Misr Bank in Beirut, which could be cashed at the Hedjaz. Only he would be able to do it there, because the woman has no capacity there. In addition, we had given a large sum of gold to a friend of Soleiman in Damascus. We were to meet this man in Oneiza, where he was riding a camel across the desert. For the time being, we had to get money here, with checks made out to Soleiman. As the poor devil could neither read nor write and no longer even had a passport with his fingerprints, it became necessary to have two witnesses to guarantee his identity. Mr. Gabbour agrees to play this role. I am dressing in European style to sign on as a second witness.

Here we are at the Banco di Roma. The formalities finished, we push in front of Soleiman a bundle of banknotes. My Bedouin, who has never seen this currency, remains mute and motionless, content to look around proudly. I take the money, but the employees don't hear it that way. They ask Soleiman if he allows me to hold his property. Everyone looks at him with respect,

Mr. Gabbour is constantly overwhelming him with the title of Emir.

Then, magnificently, Soleiman raises his brown and gold habaye and, tilting his head to my side, articulates :

– Secretary me.

The bank staff is still in a state of shock. What, an emir with a European secretary and a suite, Mrs. Amoun, Mr. Gabbour, etc.. It has such an effect that an hour later, five reporters invade the hotel to find out the identity of this sumptuous prince.

Mr. Gabbour diplomatically dismissed them with a thousand

courtesies. And we finally have peace. However, three days pass without news from the Company. I telephoned Suez who answered :

"No Passport"

Are we going to sink so close to the port ? Where is it ? It has to be in Cairo, since only there is a Nedjian consulate. Telephone again, telegram, panic... And, the day after tomorrow, as despair begins to overwhelm me, the Company brings us the paper we so much desire.

It's nine o'clock. It is March 28th. A boat leaves, it seems, Suez on the 29th. The train to Suez has just left. By car we could catch up with it at the Lidd connection. It is true that, if we have the Nedjien visa, we lack the Egyptian. However, a recent ordinance of King Fuad requires eight days to obtain the Egyptian visa.

A supreme effort, however, is possible. Mr. Gabbour, who has friendships at the Egyptian Consulate, agrees to accompany Soleiman there. I am kept informed by phone of the procedures and the remedies.

At a quarter to eleven o'clock, the wind seems good...

I rush into a car with my poor luggages, accompanied by the faithful Mrs. Amoun. We are waiting at the door of the consulate. Five past eleven... The driver goes upstairs to revive Soleiman and Mr. Gabbour. Twenty past eleven... They're coming down in a hurry, that's it.

Mrs. Amoun jumps on the ground, Soleiman jumps in the car; the visa money, which Mr. Gabbour hands me, falls out without being picked up and we start in a hurry towards the junction where we have to take the train to Suez at noon.

SUEZ

WE'RE GOING AT HIGH SPEED, IN LESS THAN forty minutes we cut down the forty-five kilometers that separate us from Lidd. It's a crazy courtyard with turns, laces, descents, breaking one's neck a hundred times. Soleiman is sick at heart.

We arrive, the train whistles, it shakes. We jump up and down on the steps of the last car, complacent people grab our suitcases and Soleiman, bewildered, exhausted, falls on a bench sighing :

– Ma'am, my head is falling off, as you always tire me.

And he falls asleep whispering: "Taben, cherol, tired, work...".

The journey is long and monotonous, sand, always sand, an arid landscape that at the beginning is enlivened by the kilometers of orange groves impeccably aligned, with large leaves so shiny that they seem to be varnished.

Jewish colonization reigns here. Only the patience of the chosen race was able to transform the desert and defeat an inexorable nature, before which generations of men had retreated. A methodical, skillful, obstinate irrigation, stubborn in its setbacks and finally triumphant, changed this desert land into a garden. The inhabitants are grouped together, with the owner or manager of the plantation acting as patriarch. Around a central farm, the labor force is gathered in small houses made of corrugated iron.

At each station, the name of the city is given in Hebrew, Arabic and English. Men and children in rags offer beautiful seedless oranges, figs, goat's milk in small black sandstone urns, hard-boiled eggs and also flowers.

Soleiman would like to buy everything, he is a sickly gourmand. I sometimes give him one of these pleasures, but I would like to stop seeing him smoke so that he doesn't spit anymore. Fortunately, smoking will be banned when we are in the countries where Ibn Saud reigns. Kantara, the customs. Traveling torment. This border post is particularly unpleasant. All my friends and I have always had problems there.

We only have a transit visa, so we are suspects. They confiscate the money we are carrying, with the promise to return it to us at the boat in Suez ! That's not all, a vaccine is missing, I could never figure out which one. We are being rushed to get it. We walk two kilometers in the sand between two nurses, to be taken to the quarantine doctor. When he sees us, he takes a huge syringe filled with a giant needle. And, as I move my leg forward, he signals that he wants to start with Soleiman.

My passport husband gets half of the vaccine in his arm, then it's my turn. I shyly ask if it would not be appropriate to change the needle. The doctor shrugs his shoulders and then the operation is done:

– Isn't he your husband ?

We have to go through the search... It's applied, I know, a little bit everywhere, but I've never been subjected to it before. In a small room, a fat woman leaves a knitted fabric behind to feel me and touch me from every angle. She finally declares herself satisfied and respectfully touches two "gris-gris" that I carry on my heart.

We pass the canal, we are at the Egyptian Kantara. Soleiman meets acquaintances. They are, in fact, friend's friend's friends...

Yet, one would think they have been linked for centuries. We have a comforting tea with these friends whose number is growing every moment. We are escorted in chorus to the train with touching wishes to our compartment, twenty cordial hands pass us our suitcases and, when the train shakes, they are desperate gestures, as if we were leaving inseparable brothers.

Here is Suez this time. It is midnight. We are exhausted. Only one idea floating in our tired brains : sleep. Soleiman is accosted by a kind of drogman who thinks he guesses the household to be exploited. My "passport husband", flattered by the consideration that the other spreads, is confused in salamalecs. I would like to put an end to this. But it is too late. Soleiman has already asked him to take us to a good hotel. No doubt, this night tout is going to lead us to a dump, but it is fortunate, in any case, that the said hotel is in front of the station. It is called the Abassiade hotel, and its painted facade seduces Soleiman. We ask the old Turk, night watchman, who stretches out blowing, for a room with two beds. The poussah asks us a fabulous price for two iron bunks, with a single sheet and a red wool cover rough as a horse blanket. Tomorrow we'll make arrangements with the boss; for the moment we only want to sleep.

Neither furniture nor table, in our house, on the ground a gargoyle of water, because the Arabs drink anything, anytime and they are always thirsty. Soleiman is satisfied, let's say that he first kindly offered me the spout, he does it ritually and I always refuse. Impossible to wash oneself well in such a lodge, it is necessary to go to the hammam, a small cemented room with a reservation for ablutions. For us Europeans, without a bathtub and a basin, washing is impossible. But the Arabs, trained in this kind of sport, do much better. We go to bed without a word. Soleiman falls asleep like a lump.

The next day, as soon as the offices opened, I was at the Navigation Company, where an employee told me that the information given in Jerusalem was wrong. No boat today 29. The next liner will leave on the 3rd or 4th. It is a cargo ship which will be in Djeddah on the 9th at dawn. This allows us to reach Mecca before noon. I am sorry to have three days to spend here, I would have been happier to spend them in Jerusalem with my so kind friends.

I'm running away from our miserable hotel. Port-Tewfik, where the canal staff lives, spreads its facades along the sea, in the shade of tall trees. It is the only shady promenade in Suez. A five-kilometer long straight road connects this modern city to the ancient Arab city. In the middle of the road is the railroad that runs all day long between Suez itself and Port-Tewfik.

Sitting under the tamarisk and eucalyptus trees, facing the sea, I read the life of Mohammed. One morning, I accept an invitation from a sailor who offers me to go fishing with him. I spend my evenings with Soleiman, we give each other French and Arabic lessons. He wants to learn how to read his own language; every time he recognizes a letter, a crazy laugh of happy child shakes him. I try all the little Arabic restaurants, I take off my veil according to the circumtances. Still dressed as an European, I go to the Navigation Company, where, with a light way, I declare :

– I come again, as you know, to get the tickets for this poor Arab who wants to go on pilgrimage with his Bedouin wife, he can't manage on his own.

Once, I am insidiously asked if it is not precisely me who wants to leave ? I am surprised.

– Don't think about it, a European woman cannot enter these countries.

And I'm leaving again without getting the tickets.

Our last night in Suez included a comic incident.

When it was time to undress me, Soleiman refused to leave our room as he usually did. In the middle of the room, crossing his arms, he stared at me with authority. I went out immediately and began to undress in the hotel lobby. As I was about to get naked, Soleiman appeared. He is dismayed and begs me to return urgently to avoid the scandal he is about to see. He apologizes and says to me submissively :

– Command, obeying you will be gentle to me.

I am glad to have the last word, it is useful that I know in advance the limits of my power over this barbarian. But is the only purpose of this new correction to make me more confident, for the time when he will be better armed : at Ibn Saud's house ?

He often alluded to it.

– You know, when we are in Oneiza, we will have to sleep in my bed.

– Do you know my conditions ?

– Yes ! but over there, my father, my mother, the slaves who will come to bring us water in the morning will have to find us on the same bed. If they found out that you are not my wife, they would kill you and the king would have my neck cut off.

– You know you don't have a bed; whether I sleep on the floor a meter or more away from you, it will be the same. No one will see any more. And then we'll see how things will turn out on the spot.

Soleiman was terrified by the severity of Ibn Saud's police in the Nedj.

MYSTICS

WE HAVE TICKETS, THE BOAT IS ANNONCED in Port-Saïd and, the next day at five o'clock, we are on the boarding dock. I took back definitively, until the far end of my adventure, my Muslim costume.

Large boats go by slowly, because there is a speed not to be exceeded, it seems, otherwise the edges, vibrating and shaken, would collapse.

A colourful crowd surrounds us. A Hindu with a strange allure and costume joins us. He is prodigiously thin and as long as a shadow. His hands look like giant spiders coming out of his sleeves. He is dressed in a royal blue frock coat with golden buttons, closed on rosewood colored pants. And his feet are wearing incredible blood-red shoes, matching the tarbouche, which is also wide open, completed by a condor's head, with a perfectly shaved skull. This sensational costume doesn't strike so much here. Colors and clothes of all kinds abound, dominated by light, airy pastel colors worn by Hindus.

A launch of the "Dandolo" approaches, flying the Italian flag. We embark, there is hardly anything around us worthy of the name "luggages". Rather, it's more like a Gypsies move : sewn bundles and cloth bags, baskets containing kitchen utensils, blackened pots, pans, primus and other unglamorous objects pile up in an astonishing bric-a-brac... All this junk sings of the poverty of this modest world.

We cross the footbridge leading to the board. We are parked like cattle, at the front. We sit among a pile of canvas stinking of grease and tar, decrepit winches, worn ropes. There are four days of crossing. We will have to live this lapse in this mess. Soleiman, who is a volunteer, advises me to go and join the women. I go there, I try to converse with one of them who seems welcoming to me. After a lot of effort, I can only assume that a woman's name is Zeinab, like mine. My namesake is lanky and skinny with piercing, rheumy eyes and a matte skin. She is draped in a black sari, embroidered with gold, but dirty, disgusting, frayed at the bottom and dusty. Her child is hidden in a sordid pile of rags. As I randomly answer affirmatively to one of her sentences, she puts the baby on my lap. I hate this smelly package. He, himself, little in sympathy, soon begins to scream.

I pass it on to his mother.

But the men suddenly run up, they have just found out that this is not the boat from Ceylon and our whole group of Hindus rush to flee by the bridge. Only the Hindu with the disproportionate size, with the impressive thinness, remains. He is in first class, but will spend all the crossing with us.

The "Dandolo" shakes gently. I leave... joy...

Here is the end of the canal and the Red Sea. Suez disappears in the distance, faded in the mist as in my memory.

Passengers are not fed on board. There are four of us, the maneuver requires at all times that we gain port and then starboard. Finally here we are on the badly joined planks of the bow wedge. A tent, that one sets up there for us, shelters us from sunstrokes. I enjoy this crossing, on the Red Sea with these strange Muslims. One of the new abayes of Soleiman's trousseau serves me as a mattress. Two suitcases delimit my bedroom... Provisions spread out, we all crouch in a circle and I leave my veil. The whole crossing will be like this.

I have cans of preserves, condensed milk, jams, mineral water, cheese, cookies and cans of cocoa. So many wonders.

However, I recommend to Soleiman to be very sober and promise myself to eat as little as possible. Wasn't the Ramadan fast created for reasons of hygiene and isn't the Koran that institutes it not our guide ? But Soleiman would like to keep his appearance of emir. He has already made countless allusions to it, and our too beggarly appearance is extremely painful for him. I make him understand that we would have immediately grasped our real situation if we were living like in the great world. I add that he must renounce his pretensions, because he cannot hold them for long. He protests.

Our two deck companions are called res- pectively : Ahmed and Mohamed.

Ahmed is a mischievous little Yemeni boy with an amazing vitality who used to be a sailor, says his passport. He has seen China, London and New York. Everywhere he's had, he says, the beautiful role, and he chatters constantly. For a bit, he would take command of the ship. He never says anything silly, and the sailors listen to his advice... but they don't follow it. His language is a surprising gibberish, a mixture of words from all the countries he has been to. Soleiman understands nothing of his thoughts, but the skinny Hindu and I follow him as best we can. He wears an original costume. A whole piece of fabric is rolled up on his head, in a voluminous turban, and a skillful draping wraps his bust to fall in harmonious folds on his knees. His gait is cadenced and elegant, he wears very large shoes with square tips, red velvet, Chinese made... Thus he already held our attention when he carried with ease, on the boarding ladder, bags of vegetables, tea and even half a sheep, the Hindu having charged him with all his commissions.

Mohamed, the impassive and silent one of our team, whispers

suras of the Koran all day long. Apart from these ritual words, I have never heard his voice.

What will fill the hours will be the religious conversations with the great Hindu who, I dare say, will truly convert me. I love this uncomfortable experience. Normal life with all its facets is boring. I hate monotony : here, I avoid it altogether. Ahmed is taking over the new position of cook and butler. He fills it perfectly and starts offering me tea in a Chinese container that holds a liter... Is it the local color, or is it my desire to be happy everywhere ? I find this tea exquisitely Chinese, Ahmed treats me like his sister, and names me "Zeinab" with delicious simplicity.

But suddenly a transparent shadow stops at the entrance of the tent, greets with a noble slow gesture, moves, and sits down in front of me. It is the Hindu, thinner than ever. This time, a simple white veil encircles his body. He inspires me with an unspoken feeling, astonishment, curiosity mixed with admiration, a kind of fascination emanates from him. Immediately he talks about God. His word is calm, soft, engaging. His conviction is so absolute, so penetrating that I am deeply moved. A contraction hugs my throat, he still speaks. It is as if he is describing a marvelous landscape.

One feels physically soothed by the quiescent and definitive tenderness that exudes from his words. It is not his logic that possesses me when he speaks to me about the religion of the Prophet, but his thoughts are so sincere, so absolute, that they are transmitted telepathically. I have never been so moved. Soleiman, who dozes off, according to his habit, finds us very talkative. We talk about eternity... The language we use is English. I don't speak enough the language to understand everything without an exhausting application. But this effort, which hypnotizes me, plays its part in the mysticism that is born in me.

I am learning a thousand things. First of all, that everything is in the

Koran, including the best ways of governing. It is in truth an encyclopedia, a code, an administrative, political and military law. This explains the judicial, moral and political similarity of all Muslim countries under all skies.

The legal principles and the laws that result from them are, in fact, immutable. The Prophet has established what no parliament, no monarchy, no representative of any government can then change. Islam enters into the details of daily life with such rigor that no one can free himself from its prescriptions, which become reflexes in the long run.

Islam is a religion of submission to which no one thinks of escaping. Its imprint seems unalterable, although one can observe some modifications in details brought by Western civilization in these countries. Thus, contrary to what one might think, the veil for women is not an institution of the Koran. Aisha, Mohamed's favoured wife, and her daughter Fatima used to take part in discussions with men or even follow them to war with their faces uncovered. The Koran simply says, "Women should be modest and cover certain parts of their bodies (not including the face) and do nothing that can get the attention of men". It was only after the death of the Prophet that the custom of veiling oneself became an obligation for women. In recent years, the growing influence of the West has led to the abolition of the veil in several Islamic countries, such as Turkey and, to some extent, Egypt.

I was struck, in all our conversations and in the deeper knowledge that resulted for me, by the similarities that can be observed between Christianity and Islam. The Muslim believes, like the Christian, in heaven, hell, eternal rewards, the Last Judgment. A rather important difference results from the Muslim belief in a single god, surrounded by prophets such as Abraham, Moses, Christ, Mohammed, while Christians put the saints in collaboration with God, by praying them and making use of their intercession. No Muslim addresses himself to

Muhammed, all their prayers go directly to Allah.

As among Catholics, the Muslim religion does not recommend forgiveness of offenses. The best is the one who reconciles first.

We discussed religion in the evenings until it was time to go to sleep. For hours, I listen to the Hindu saying things that disturb me infinitely.

The calm sea, the somewhat abstract scenery, the extraordinary personality of the Hindu gave me during these few days an absolute moral rest, a complete detachment from the things of this world, the perfect happiness, if it exists in this world. It is difficult to analyze, but I think I found there the only hours of serenity and spiritual peace that life has brought me so far.

The Hindu, during the two years he has been in London, has not consumed any food prepared by "unfaithful" hands. In countries of great civilization where this is difficult to observe, he ate only raw fruits and vegetables.

Here again, sobriety is essential, because Ahmed, despite all his skill, has only basic means. His exquisite tea, which we consume in large quantities, radically spoils the appetite. A few kind sailors brought me a warm bun on the last day. It seemed succulent to me.

We prayed together, under the guidance of the Hindu, who said them first, with a recollection and holiness that took him out of the world. Ahmed's prayers, on the other hand, were incredibly imaginative... It was not long before the rumbling he filled the prayers with made me burst out laughing. The crew, surprised, often came to attend these mystical manifestations, some surrounded us with respect, others with irony.

People on the boat had come to know that I was a French woman, under my Bedouin appearance. Officers and sailors came, sometimes, to have a conversation with me. They did it in secret, fearing Muslim fanaticism. The commander also offered me to use his bathroom. One day, seeing me going there, Soleiman pretended to use it. I put him in his place, and told him all my regrets for not having married a simple, clever and resourceful guy like Ahmed, he had a violent resentment.

The director of the Massaoua saltworks, who was there and with whom I would sometimes converse in Spanish, hated Soleiman and considered him a scary savage under his soft mask. He wanted me to write to him from time to time, knowing what I pretended to do in Arabia, to prove to him that I had not been killed.

– This is my address, he said. If I don't hear from you in a fortnight, you will have been murdered.

I had, for some reason, the feeling of a threat of death on my head. But this impassive sky, this scorching sun, this smooth sea brought me to accept it without bitterness and without regrets.

The curiosity that inspires my need to travel and to change horizons without respite made my mind constantly cross the limits of material life. The unknown of death fascinated me. So I did not apprehend anything. But I realized that my present bliss could come from a possible foreknowledge of the confessions and an intuition of the supreme deliverance that accompanies the revelation of the last secret. Every evening, leaning against the rail, without desire or ulterior motives, I watch the star fall into the distance. My moral pride is so intense that my physical appearance is influenced by it. Total, immaterial well-being... is it ecstasy ?

Reality always takes back its rights. We will arrive in Djeddah, Ahmed takes care of our pilgrim costumes. The luggage of the Hindu is, on this subject, our resource to all of us. Soleiman will find there the terry cloth to girdle the kidneys and cover the left shoulder while leaving the right shoulder naked, which is a ritual in pilgrimage. The head and feet must remain naked for the men.

DJEDDAH

DJEDDAH, IT IS THE DOOR OF ISLAM believer. Whoever goes to Mecca and is received by Djeddah must fulfill various obligations, all of them religious.

One must first put on the *irham, the* pilgrimage outfit, shave, cut one's nails and ablue one's body; this creates a state of physical purity comparable to the moral one which must, in the Catholic religion, follow confession and precede communion. Pilgrims should no longer have sexual intercourse, not even touching a woman's hand.

One must also avoid killing any beast, including the most nagging parasite. He will no longer cut his nails, shave, or have his hair cut during the trip to Mecca. He will not pluck a single blade of grass, nor a leaf, if he wants to remain pure; since God gives him life, he is forbidden to remove it. In sacred places, it is a sin to hunt a fly that lands on your face. Women on pilgrimage are completely covered from head to toe with a white sheet; only two holes for the eyes are allowed.

Ahmed finds precisely in the suitcases of the Hindu a vast piece of cotton. I make a bag of it for myself, and with my scissors I make the two permitted holes. As my companions inquire about my outfit, I pass it around with a triumphant laugh, but then I see only disapproving faces. All declare that I am dressed inappropriately; the bottom of the bag must sweep the dust and I have shortened, so that it is possible for me to move forward, this dress which bothered me. I return it to a congruent length and I have to pierce the eye hole much higher than I had done. I don't know if now I will see where I can walk, but it will be God's will.

At dawn, we see the floating buoys indicating the entrance to the religious area. The prayers begin. Everyone thanks Allah for the prodigious favor that will be the fulfillment of the pilgrimage.

As Djeddah has nothing worth seeing in detail, we decide to take a car with the five of us to reach Mecca urgently. It is time if we want to reach the sacred mountain of El Arafat today.

But these are futile decisions and my hopes will be dashed.

It is five o'clock in the morning, the boat stops in open sea, far from the coast. Through the spyglass we see the white Djeddah, made of penthouses.

The facades are loaded with "moucharabiehs" made of wood from the islands of the Indian Ocean. These are contributions from Javanese Mohammedans, who paid the price of their visit to the holy places.

Around Djeddah, not a tree, not a blade of vegetation. It is the desert. There, behind some distant hills, lies Mecca.

The Djeddah bay is deserted almost all year round. But at the time of Islamic devotions it was filled with enormous activity. Great international liners are currently anchored there. All the Muslim races of the world have arrived in these ships : Sudanese, blue-eyed Berbers, Hindus, Africans, Malays, slaves from all the countries where there are still slaves, abound. Close to the coast, a ship's carcass shows the catastrophe suffered by the liner Asia in the past. Ahmed Muslem wants to frighten us by telling us how the French officers of this ship were executed by Ibn Saud for having caused the death of hundreds of pilgrims by imperialism. It is true that the news is upset, but I hear Soleiman, no doubt to redeem the crime of having married a "roumi", say that it was well deserved.

A speedboat brings us the harbor master and Dr. Yaya, for the usual formalities. They are both dressed in tussor robes and *kéfié (1)* made of canvas. The whole dazzling whiteness. They have varnished pumps and wear gold chains. In this place, both give an impression of richness and refinement.   Let us say that Djeddah, which is subject to Ibn Saud, Puritan king of the Nedj, was conquered by him in 1926.

Until then the Hijaz had been subject to Ali Hussein, brother of Faisal, former king of Iraq. Ibn Saud possesses in any case at this time nine tenths of Arabia and is about   to take the rest.

Let's resume our story... The commander, having made the necessary examinations and accomplished the classical formalities, makes the pilgrims parade in front of him; the men pass, then me, the only woman, quite far behind. We are ordered to embark on the launch. I crouch in front of it. Doctor Yaya, in his turn, asks everyone : "What is your name, your country, are you married, is this your first pilgrimage?

Mohamed answers that he was born in Mecca and simply returns home, where he will end his life in prayer.

The Hindu, still in ecstasy, answers politely but barely.

The others, Ahmed and Soleiman, are more exu-berants. The latter stands out for its stupidity :

– I just got married to a French woman I bring back from Syria.

The doctor slowly asks him if he thinks his wife will be able to get used to Oneiza's life.

(1) Kéfié, veil covering the head.

– Of course it will have to, doesn't she have to follow me everywhere ?

I am meanwhile on the burning coals, I contain my anger and seem not to have heard anything.

But Dr. Yaya finally turns to me. He expresses himself in perfect French :

– Are you French ?

– I am, or rather I was.

– Do you plan to stay in this country for a long time ?

– I mainly come to visit it and meet my in-laws from Oneiza. Then, in three or six months at the latest, we will leave again.

– How will you endure this existence ?

– I have already led the same life in Syria with the Bedouins. I love this primitive and patriarchal life.

– Do you intend to make the pilgrimage ?

– Certainly, it will be a great joy for me, as a Muslim of yesterday, to approach Allah's sanctuary and receive his graces. I will be proud to bear the title of Hedje Zeinab.

Yaya withdraws into an icy impassivity.

Sometimes a coral reef is hooked and the propeller wedges. But finally we arrive and disembark.

At the customs, Dr. Yaya asked me to follow him for a short while. The men are waiting for me to take the road to El Arafat as soon as possible.

With the doctor, I go up a series of small green stairs, then I enter a large room, furnished with a desk on which a telephone is placed.

A digression here, because the mixture of extreme civilization and primitive simplicity that characterizes this country will surprise the reader.

King Ibn Saud, of surprising intelligence, is an enemy of too great a civilization in itself, but he takes useful inventions from it to his plans as an omnipotent ruler who wants to be everywhere and quickly obeyed.

Tobacco and alcohol are forbidden in his home. Caught drinking arak, Arabs were sentenced to six months in prison, plus a hundred strokes on the first of each month... They talk about wine there as an evil and odious drug.

On the other hand, cars and telephones are in common use.

I'm not worried right now, but I'm curious. Dr. Yaya sits at his desk and continues to question me. I do my best to avoid any missteps.

Finally, he is silent. I think he wants a medical visit and I offer to take my clothes off. He seems surprised. I ask if he wants to look at my vaccinations.

My companions, I said finally, are waiting for me to begin the pilgrimage.

He then offers me a cup of tea and, looking straight at me,

slowly articulates that he fears he can't let me go.

I ask him emotionally about the reason for such an obstacle,

– It is that you are French.

– I am Nedjian by my marriage, Muslim too. I have to follow my husband everywhere.

– You are right in this, but the law requires every new convert to practice Islam for two years before entering Mecca.

– Like Nedjian I can go to Mecca without even being converted, don't you know it ?

However, the doctor doesn't want to decide anything. He phoned the deputy governor of Djeddah who also does not want to accept any responsibility. The king, the ministers and the Emir of Djeddah left for El Arafat. It will be impossible to join them and have a decision before three days.

The conversation is over. Dr. Yaya concludes that the Deputy Governor, the only person who could have allowed me to leave, is absolutely opposed to it until further notice.

– Your friends have now left for Mecca.

our husband must have followed them, he told me, in the end.

The deputy governor is visibly suspicious of me.

Only one unfaithful person, sneaking among thousands of pilgrims, cancels all the graces of the pilgrimage and for all. I wanted to do without the French consulate. Indeed, I know from experience that consular officials everywhere have only one idea: that of stopping the desires of their nationals, to avoid the complications that could result for them.

But I have no choice.

I ask the doctor to take me to the consul of my country.

He answers me coldly

– Never ! Muslim woman, you must not have any more relationship with these people.

I made a terrible mistake.

I then try to get to the hotel. I would like to regain some of my compromised freedom.

The answer is inflexible.

– A Muslim woman should not go alone to a hotel.

– Where am I going to go since, according to you, everything is told to me ?

He begs me to be patient and starts calling again. I don't know what he's saying or to whom.

But I understand that he is looking for a harem to house me. Finally, he ended by saying that the family of the deputy governor accepted me and that they would take me to his house.

Under escort, I leave in an infinite maze of small dirt alleys. They are identically narrow, dark and deserted. It is that everyone is on pilgrimage. Here we are in front of a monumental door, framed by lanterns hanging on the wall and similar to two street lamps. The door is wide open, as in all Arab houses in Djeddah. A swarm of crouching slaves and servants await the visitor, they are dressed in fancy clothes, some in short dresses, trailing dresses with sleeves so long and flared that, to work, some have raised their pointed ends, tied on the neck. Their heads are shaved. They wear either a kéfié, or a small white cloth cap, in cone, "kofia", which miraculously holds on the occiput.

The deputy governor waits on a step of the stairs, dressed in white, with a plain veil kéfié.

In each region of Islam, the kéfiés have a particular character in Baghdad, for example, the fabric, with a white background, has red or black checks in relief. Here, it is finer and simpler.

The man has big black curls around his, very matt and brown face. His look from the start is soft, but extremely sneaky. Without a word, with a simple gesture, he invites me up. The steps are high and the slope steep. I finally find myself on the third floor, in a small room closed by a moucharabieh. I slump down next to a very strong woman. I am locked in a harem.

THE HAREM

I FIND MYSELF IN A ROOM WITHOUT furniture. In front of the moucharabieh, however, is a kind of wide step, covered with an old carpet : the couch. Within the walls are niches without symmetry. Here are piles of blankets and rows of tiny glass blocks. For the custom in Hijaz is to drink tea continuously. Such containers will change me from Ahmed's glass, which contained a liter... The covers are for the night. However, the fat woman receives me and tilts her head with an obvious gravel. She touches her forehead and utters a few words that I can't hear and that I can't answer. But she makes a gesture that enlightens, if I may say so, my religion. She wants me to take off my pilgrimage garment, the white bag that covers me completely. I hesitate about what to do, then, after refusing, I don't know why, I consent. So here I am in my underwear. I wait anxious and angry, what will happen to me unexpectedly and that I fear a little.

It is barely ten o'clock in the morning. Slave women enter. They laugh, point at me and come to touch me like an unknown animal. They also want to see if I am a woman like the others... They chatter together, loudly and vertiginously. Their Arabic is so different from the Syrian Arabic that I don't understand them at all. Time passes very slowly. It is already the life of a harem, and I am waiting. Waiting for what ? God only knows. I have a headache and I'm starving. Finally, around three o'clock in the evening I am brought a fatty and sour liquid on a plate, where green herbs are swimming. It's filthy and I can't swallow anything despite my desire. Luckily the tea is good, even better, exquisite. And I drink as much of it as I am offered. Often... The huge woman goes out and comes back again and again. It is visible that she wants to please me and does her best. Constantly she repeats, shouting, as well as a refrain, the formula so well known :

– Enta mabsout ? ana mabsout.

(Are you happy ? If so, I'm happy.)

I don't answer anything at first. Yet it is too certain that it annoys me, then, exasperated I shout :

– But no, I'm not happy. I have a headache, I have been separated from my husband and I can't go on the pilgrimage.

– Malesh, she answers in turn. Which means, at the same time, what to do about it ? and never mind ! I am, she adds, even angrier than you are. It's been ten years since I've missed a single visit to the holy places.

But this year, the duty was to stay, as my son-in-law had kept his wife in Djeddah with him.

She explains to me, with an air of great importance, that she is the mother-in-law of the deputy governor, Ali Allmari. But, as he has already lost four wives, she no longer dares to leave her daughter. She wants to make me feel and share her contempt for Djeddah, a miserable city, without comfort, without cinema, without photographer.

For in Basra, her country of origin, she has experienced all the refinements of high civilization. Here, by order of the king, no modern entertainment is allowed in Hijaz or Nedj. And, out of respect for the Koran, one sentence of which condemns material reproductions of nature, photography itself is forbidden.

All the men in command here are Wahabites, like the king, who led the movement to drive out the family of Sheriff Hussein. Wahabism dates from the second half of the 18th century. It is a doctrine which aim is to return Islam to its primitive purity. In particular, it rejects the cult of the marabouts, so dear to North Africa, and all that seems to awaken the old cult of Eve, whose alleged tomb was once in Djeddah. This tomb of the mother of men was thus destroyed by order of Ibn Saud.

And, even in front of the tomb of the Prophet, the visitor should refrain from all demonstrations that would resemble the devotion of a worship only reserved to Allah.

In fact, Ibn Saud obeys rather than commits himself to this harsh puritanism. He certainly observes it, but with real liberalism. And even this is the reproach that he constantly incurs from the Wahabites of strict observance : that of opportunism. For a puritan always finds more puritan than himself, and one of his great vassals, Faisal Ed Daouich, chief of the Moutayr tribe, rose up against Ibn Saud three years ago in protest against the king's opportunism. This aggressive and ascetic figure had, in the event of victory, decided to deliver Mecca to massacre and plunder for three days. After that, the survivors would have gathered together to make amends for their sins in public...

If we see there how Faisal Ed Daouich would have treated the most faithful of his co-religionists and the city, the holiest of Islam, "the mother of cities", we can guess how he thought he would act towards Europeans ...

Luckily, Ibn Saud defeated him and put him in the shade for two years at the bottom of a silo.

Now I must say that Soleiman just belonged to the Moutayr tribe, "Birds of Prey". It is the wildest of the center of the Nedj.

These reflections are made only to make the king of the Nedj sympathetic, in contrast to the "pure man" bloodsuckers of the kingdom.

Ibn Saud is a man of the first order, who is admired for his intelligence, his energy and the rules of pure life that he faithfully follows.

Coming back to my fat friend, her name is Kadija. She is nobly called only Sett Kebir, which means Great Mistress, she is descended from the Cherif, and she insists that I have an exact account of this marvelous filiation.

I want to be pleasant to her and acknowledge her great nobility. She goes on to explain to me her kinship with Ali Hussein, the former king of Hedjaz. Now that everyone is reassured about me and that the slaves have contemplated me at their ease, it is the turn of the women of the harem to come and see me. Sett Kebir's daughter is the first. She wears a white muslin dress, with satin stripes. Her beautiful hands hang down along her body. Her fragranced hair falls in long braids on both sides of her head.

She meticulously follows the hedja-zian code of politeness, takes my hand, carries it to her forehead and finally kisses it. Her name is Fakria, she is the wife of the deputy governor. She is sixteen years old and has been married for eight years.

She has a six-year-old daughter following her, holding two pretty children with a scrawny face and transparent skin. They are the daughters of one of Ali Allmari's missing wife. The last of the women's parade is Mousny. While many others are almost deformed from fat, none are as thin and perfectly made as this black girl. Her interior outfit appears charming : a small vest very tight on the loins, made of cotton muslin, revealing ravishing breasts, with puffy pants, whose fullness is brought back from behind.

Her air is lively, intelligent and attentive. One can guess that she recognizes herself as being superior to other black women. She is the result of a weakness of the sub-gouverner for a slave. However, as a recognized daughter, she is now entitled to the same consideration as all the others. They meet in a semi-circle in front of me, and exchange words that at other times would amuse me :

– How small her eyes are

– And her hands, how tiny they are !

– What a strange white skin

– Does she have a Muslim heart ?

Other curious women have now joined the circle around me and are inciting the wives of the deputy governor to doubt my heart. But the subject of the curiosity changes. What interests them now is to know if I am made like them in every detail of my body...

They approach me with a smile and touch me with a lascivious simplicity, so meticulous that, disgusted and furious, I repel them strongly. Later, in front of the insistent curiosity of one of them, the neighbor Selma, I even break her wrist defending myself, which makes quite a deal, because the kind of indiscretion that made me react cannot be confessed to men.

The day ends slowly. Sett Kébir, to whom I tell my weariness and my need to sleep, nobly points out the ground, like a castellan that would lead you to the beautiful guest room...

I look melancholically at this thin and worn carpet. The slaves are wearing some blankets. In this same room, several other women go to sleep too. I finally lie down, exhausted. Others do the same, but there are some who meet in a corner. In the light of a lantern they go to chat all night long. At two o'clock in the morning, as all Islam does, Sett Kebir gets up and makes her prayers and ablutions.

I don't move, my dismay is too great. At dawn, I wake up, broken by aches and pains, my head heavy and more exhausted than the day before. At nine o'clock, the slaves bring the el fatour, breakfast made up of home-made bread, sour and dirty goat white cheese, on which, today, the letters of the newspaper that wrapped it are printed, then onions, raw leeks, with roots and green stems, which must be eaten from the top, and finally white beans, covered with rancid sheep butter (smen).

Bread has the shape of a round cake. Low-rised, made of barley flour and sea water.

Hard to swallow these horrors Then I ask to wash myself.

But Fakria, with a kind of irony, still kindly declares that the common hammam must not be suitable enough for my use.

She then makes me climb into hers, which goes beyond the limits of common comfort : there is, in fact, a bucket of sea water and a bucket of fresh water, with the small bowl used to water the body...

Because, let's not forget, the water that has touched the lower parts of the body must never come into contact with the upper parts.

Muslim law, which is not a joke, effectively requires that I start pouring water on my shoulders, then my stomach, then my thighs and finally my feet. Washing oneself, which is called washing in the West, becomes here, with this obligatory ritual, one of the most difficult problems.

I'm doing the best I can, and when I come back, Sett Kebir said to me with anointing :

– I hear that you have committed a sin again !

– Why this ?

– A slave watched you through the skylight in the doorway. You did not wash yourself according to the rite. And then, there is something serious...

– But what else?

– You're not depilated.

I am startled, she continues.

– Yes, and we wonder how your husband can tolerate you like this, because you are not a true Muslim.

I guess the words do not convey the full intensity of the scandal I just caused. But, as I am lying on the couch, hoping for peace, I see them all, after a religious conciliatory, come to me, and ask to see...

An indignation takes them in front of the living blasphemy that constitutes this hair system... and they immediately set to work, to get me into the rule : with tweezers and, if needed, their fingers, with a sugar syrup that hardens and forms a block that is pulled out in one go with the hair...

They hurt me terribly and their fever is so high, their desire to succeed so urgently, that they remove my skin.

I am defending myself badly by telling them that their idea of mixing religion with such trivia is strictly ridiculous. Since faith is in my heart, the hairs on my body don't change anything. I no longer have the strength to fight; moreover, I understand that I must not make enemies of these women. ignorant, naive and of such original modesty.

Then, with a razor, I finish the operation started by so many painful means. Sett Kebir insidiously asks me if Soleiman is so similar to me. I answer yes and I guess then that I have dealt a final blow to my husband's prestige.

– Finally, let's not talk about all this anymore, I say, I'm going to wash again.

I go back to the hammam. I still use fresh water there. It is expensive, because there is not a drop of it in Djeddah. The king has brought machines for distilling sea water. They work day and night and the water obtained is sold in tanakés or eighteen-liter cans of gasoline. They bring this to you when you wake up, just as the milkman brings your milk to you in France. This water is poured into tanks located at the entrance of each harem, and the bill is paid at the end of the month. Once this washing is finished, Fakria is willing to admit that I look like all the women of the Eastern harem. She will do me the honors of the house. We circulate freely because the men are in Mecca.

On the first floor and on the second floor are large rooms for men's meetings, "Mejless".

On the second floor, apartments, of course without furniture, serve as guest rooms. The guests may be strangers passing through.

The harem occupies the third floor. In the fourth lives the deputy governor of Djeddah. An incredible luxury (everything is relative) is spread out there : an iron bed with bed base and mattress... There are no sheets, because Ali Allmari is unaware of the use of these objects.

But there is also a cupboard with two mirrors.

On the top floor is the terrace that covers any Arab house.

It is, in short, the only place where women can stand free and unveiled, in the open air. The terraces even serve as a link between the harems. The houses are so close together, in fact, that one can converse from one to the other and even pass objects.

One can exchange words from house to house through the moucharabiehs, because the harems are all on the same floor, in order to avoid the slightest relationship between man and woman from one house to another.

My life gradually took on a new aspect, graceless and flabby as is the very existence of the oriental woman. But I did not have the vocation. At the end of two days, not being able any more of this internment, I asked to go out to buy fabrics, to dress like other women. For I had nothing but the black dress I was wearing, under the white bag, when I arrived in Djeddah.

Sett Kebir, calmly, answers that everyone is in Mecca and that the souks are closed. I insist; she promises to accompany me when the slave has finished sweeping. Then the dishes have to be washed, then it's lunch, the heat, the night. Of course, I am sequestered, in spite of the Arab courtesy that surrounds me. I meditate on how to get out in secret. But I am never left alone. In addition, four or five slaves guard the front door.

ROYAL PALACE

NOTHING TO DO, I HAVE TO WAIT FOR THE return, still uncertain, of Soleiman.

But, oh surprise ! One morning Sett Kébir comes to tell me that we are going to go out together. I was astonished. Then, I think I need money. I'm going to ask the deputy governor for some.

He gives me, against a few pounds, a heap of Hijazi money. The English pound is worth twenty reals, and the real twenty krouchs. A teacup or tanaké of water sells for one krush. This currency, as we can see, has a great purchasing power, since for example a meter of cloth is worth two to four kruchs.

We go out. Our indoor clothes are covered with a black skirt and a small similar collar which covers the head. It also maintains the double veil of black Georgette crepe hiding the face. This collar, making a cape, falls to the hips and hides the hands. For one cannot show one's hands without sinning.

I, without thinking about it, let my arms hang down and Sett Kébir is outraged. Slaves make us procession and guide us, because none of the women of Ali Allmari's wives knows the maze of the city's alleyways.

We leave Djeddah by the gate of Mecca and walk by the sea.

Sett Kébir then showed me a huge white house with a central

veranda and twelve front windows with green shutters, like a large villa in the Paris suburbs. It is Koseir el Ardar, which belongs to Ali Allmari and is used as a dwelling for King Ibn Saud when he comes here. The furniture is a property of sovereign.

We enter this palace through a huge carriage entrance. We quickly cross the lower part, which is reserved for men, as usual.

At the first, we fall into a large patio, whose walls and columns are painted green. The floor is paved with black and white tiles, on which I am constantly scratching, they are poorly joined and we are barefoot inside.

I am devoutly shown the royal bedroom. The women are convinced, as well as the slaves, that I have never seen anything so beautiful in my life.

I can't hold back my cheerfulness in front of a silvery metal bed with an oval glass at the head and electrical lamps to all four studs. A bed canopy, also silver, drops mechanical embroidery tulle curtains. The mattress is without a sheet. And this comical splendor gives an idea of the mix that leads to the initiation of Europe in the East. In a corner, a large mirror cabinet, complete with a matching chest of drawers, then chairs and armchairs covered in bright green plush.

We then go to see the room of Emir Faisal, the son of Ibn Saud, who should not be confused with Faisal, King of Iraq, whose tragic end is known.

One finds there, as in a furniture storefront, a wardrobe with two mirrors, a varnished bed in burr walnut, a chest of drawers, and on all this a profusion of bronzes, designed in the most "Decorative Arts 1925" style.

The furniture of the living room was purchased in a department store in Constantinople. Armchairs, chairs and sofas are made of gilded wood, covered with blue and gold laminate. The natives, who have never seen anything so splendid, are literally flabbergasted by these dazzling things.

Electric wires hang in all rooms. I ask Sett Kebir if they will offer us, in addition, an illumination.

She answers, indignant

– You don't think about it. The house would be in danger of burning down. Such follies are only attempted during the king's stay.

What strikes me are the moucharabieh free windows with European-style shutters. As we cannot look out of the windows, for fear of being seen by men, we gather together, unveiled, in the patio.

The visit is over, I think we'll leave soon. But they bring us a big samovar and some dishes with various food. There are tasteless zucchinis, cut and water boiled, mutton meat, rice and bamias (Greek horns), sweet and sticky, accompanied by a brown or tomato sauce. We eat as it should be, taking the consistent pieces from the dish with our hands, and we sponge the sauce with pieces of bread...

This is how the king eats, crouching on the ground with his retinue.

I admire this biblical simplicity, but I don't like it. In fact, I keep getting dirty, either with the sauce or by the falling pieces of meat, which I don't hold firmly enough. In addition, I burn myself, because everything has been presented boiling hot. I would like to help myself before everyone, including slaves with dirty hands, has dipped their fingers in the dishes.

I soon say that I am no longer hungry, because I am disgusted to see them all grinding and manipulating what they offer me with affability.

Here is the night at last. So we will stay in the palace, and maybe spend several days there, without changing our clothes or dress. New torment. I protest at the idea of sleeping on the floor, when next door we have the king's comfortable bed, and I ask Sett Kebir if her grand-daughter Lotfia could not sleep there with me.

This proposal, which seems to me to be full of innocence, causes general indignation.

– It would be, they all shout, an immense sin.

It doesn't seem certain to me and I discuss, and remind them that the deputy governor sleeps in Faycal's room.

But they say that the son of a king is a secondary person. He is not the only one of his kind, and one has to imagine what protocol would be unthinkable if the children, grand children and great-grandchildren of Ibn Saud's three hundred wives were to be considered worthy of major respect.

I see that my intention must be abandoned. Everything I propose scandalizes these poor simple women, lost in the prejudices of six thousand years ago. I live only in sin, and, as all gestures, words, and deeds are governed by religious law, I do not wag my little finger without impiety.

An example : the right hand is made only to eat, and the left to wash. Sin (haram) to forget it...

It is necessary to have square nails, to file them almond : haram.

But Allah is merciful. Otherwise I will be a thousand and one thousand times damned.

The next day, as the noise of our presence in the palace spread, friends of my friends came to visit us. They are dressed in a very entertaining way : over the pants and the classic small indoor vest, they put on princess dresses, very tight, and dragging on the ground; the dresses are white and make them look like outdated first communicants.

The tall elegant women wear artificial silk in bright shades, especially yellow and pale blue.

All bend under the gold jewelry : from bracelets on arms and ankles, rings to every toe, chains to massive rings, necklaces and earrings.

To go out, they have corkscrew stockings, and mediocre varnished shoes; they raise, then, on the hips the colorful dress which is covered with the classical black skirt ...

The head is veiled again and the little cape shelters their hands. The little girls are, in reduction, dressed like women. Same princess dress, a small silk handkerchief is fixed on the heart by a pin, and they are covered with light and golden toy jewelry. Their hats are toques, with the classic feather. But it is used to chase away the evil eye

All these Arabic costumes, dresses or pants, have huge yards of fabric. Because of the heat, one should avoid wearing tight-fitting clothes, which would be plated by perspiration. For the same reason, one removes socks and shoes at home, and one lives barefoot in all the harems.

Children of both sexes stay with the women until the age of ten or twelve, after which the boys leave and have no further contact with them. And, to avoid encounters between different sexes, inside the harems people clap their hands as soon as they walk down the stairs, so that the male slaves leave in a hurry. A comprehensive code governs these claps.

I spend the next day looking out the window at the sea and the legations.

Their grouping has its purpose because, eighteen years ago, all the staff, even indigenous, of the French Consulate was massacred. It makes a great impression on me.

It is a small corner of civilization where the most diverse countries fraternize in the midst of a foreign atmosphere. All those who have muslim nationals have a consulate or a legation. I see nine of them, which I recognize by their flag.

Here are : the USSR, Holland, Persia, England, Italy, Egypt, Turkey, Iraq and, finally, I distinguish the French consulate, still unknown to me, and which, until then, inspired me only with mistrust, so much so that I still feared new setbacks with the civil servants whom my experiences in Syria had taught me to despise.

TELEPHONE

I'M STILL LOOKING AT THE CONSULATE OF FRANCE, my eyes are stinging. The anguish takes me out of my isolation. I see myself more and more sequestered. A mad desire seizes me to reestablish a link with my own, and to have there a means to make myself understood, which becomes more and more difficult in this harem. Now, in spite of everything, I wonder if I might find in this mysterious consulate a source of comfort. But how do I make contact and inform it of my presence in Djeddah and from being sequestered ? All my attempts to get out have failed. One is wary, indeed.

Now I see a telephone at the end of the patio ! Streak of light. I ask Fakria, who appears to be monitoring the phone, permission to use it.

She answers :

– It is broken.

I do not insist. The same day, around noon, I hear the ringing. I am simply forbidden to use it, with the suppleness and astonishing power of the polite and smiling lie that characterizes Orientals.

I decide to use this phone, whatever the cost, and watch carefully for the right moment.

Around four o'clock, everyone takes a nap. That's the minute to choose. I silently approach the device.

The anguish makes me gasp, I stammer in Arabic the word "consulate", pronouncing it in different ways, to be understood for sure. I add : "French" and repeat the word with different arabic accents, and I feel that I finally have the password.

A voice answers and questions.

I say in French, with a beating heart

– I would like to speak to Mr. Maigret.

At the end of the line there is an obvious surprise. I am tensed by fear. And, without wasting time in explanations, I stutter hastily :

– Come to my rescue. Quickly. A French woman is a prisoner at the King's palace in Koseir El Ardar...

The voice whispers :

– I am the son of Mr. Maigret. I'm going to look for you; but I don't know where the palace is.

– It is a large white house, with green shutters, built on the sand along the track of Medina.

Then I hear footsteps and voices. I hang up.

It is Fakria who asks me what I am doing.

I shrug my shoulders :

– I contemplate the telephone, it amuses me.

Then I will look out the window through the shutters. Time passes, I get nervous. I venture to say now, in a defiant way, that, dead or alive, naked or dressed, I will soon go to the French consulat. They take on an air of pity, as if in front of a madwoman :

– How would you do it, since you don't even know the way ?

I answer that I saw the French flag through the window, and knowing the direction, I will know how to find the road. Seeing me so stubborn in this revolt, they run to warn the deputy governor. He arrives at once, and tells me with courtesy that Soleiman has entrusted me to him. So he cannot take the responsibility of allowing a muslim woman to visit Christians.

I understand that, but I retort :

– It doesn't matter, I have some difficulties to clarify with the consulat, and I can't explain them to you in Arabic. So I have to go. Besides, I made an arrangement with Soleiman, which he must have told you about; he must leave me very free every day, so I will go there.

Then the Deputy Governor tells me that it is completely forbidden. I immediately revealed to him, as a precaution, that I had telephoned the consul, who was waiting for me. If I don't go to his appointment, he will be unhappy and will come to get me.

The argument is strong. The consuls have, indeed, a very great prestige near the king. Thus the beaten slaves threaten to go and complain to the consuls without even knowing which one... And, when they run away, the doors are closed, we hang on to them, they are asked to stay until they finally condescend to them with height... They know very well that, freed, they would have no more means of living.

However, this worn-out simulacrum still produces its little effect. It is true that male slaves have sometimes accomplished this threat to the end. The consulates of France or England have sent them back to their country of origin.

The Deputy Governor senses the delicate situation. He finally makes up his mind, and grants me to go to the French consulate, accompanied by two slaves. But I have to promise that I will be back in half an hour. I left and arrived at the legation. It's a large stone building. The building is surmounted by a small covered wooden platform, which is accessed by a sort of ladder.

The windows are in moucharabiehs. A vast entrance. The main door is iron clad. Against the walls, long wooden benches are at the disposal of pilgrims who are waiting for visas for their passports to return home.

Mr. M... receives me very kindly. He is a charming man, extremely intelligent, with broad and clear ideas. He is surprised to see me in the strange situation I am in at the moment. He even advises me, if I may, not to go any further on my journey.

He seriously warned me that once in the Nedj, in the interior, no intervention would be possible for him.

He still tells me the frightening difficulty of crossing the Hofouf desert, where quicksand has taught so many caravans. That the water reserves are miscalculated and death is inevitable.

I tell him my goals : to go to Mecca and Medina, by car, then, by foot, in a caravan, to Oneiza. This is the center of Arabia, where the Moutayr tribe reigns, and I will find my husband's family there. After a rest of fifteen days, I would finally like to cross the Hofouf desert, a thousand kilometers, to the Persian Gulf, where I want to fish for pearls. My husband Soleiman's brother-in-law does this job there, in the Bahrain Islands. The consul is undoubtedly right to tell me the difficulties of carrying out all this. But I will not change my decision. I say that Soleiman is in Mecca.

I am waiting for his return. If we have the king's permission, we will then attempt to carry out my plan.

I give the consul the address of my in-laws in Oneiza. If I haven't returned in six months, he can find out my fate.

The interview is over, I leave. My return to the harem is under happy auspices. I no longer feel the anguish of isolation and I feel completely reassured.

Pierre d'Andurain in military costume

Major Sinclair, Chief of
Intelligence service

Soleiman el Dikmari of the
Moutayr tribe, "Birds of prey"

The Zenobia Hotel in 1927

110

Zeïnab bent Maksime (Marga d'Andurain) and her new husband,
Soleiman in Haifa

Zeïnab in Djeddah in the costume of the harem

LIFE IN A HAREM

AND THE DAYS GO BY. I WEAR OUT THE TIME. Sett Kébir, with whom I chatted at length, has all her jewelry brought in a horrible little gusseted suitcase, as used by country doctors.

She opens it with dignity and I see a multitude of small boxes and bottles of pharmacy, in which are stored her treasures. In a biscuit box, given to her by the Iraqi consul, are large ankle bracelets; the rings are always in pairs, one for each member.

The rings have a waxing boot as a case, then they are baroque pearls, medium size, strung in large twists, and held by a single cord that serves as a closure in the back. In a box of purgative pills, series of solid gold earrings are very elaborate.

The woman's social status depending on of the importance and value of her jewelry, as I have none, which is incomprehensible to a young bride, these poor women find it very difficult to form an opinion of my rank.

The subject of physical love is inexhaustible here in the conversation; we wonder about the intimate parts of husbands, about their way of proceeding, and mainly about the enjoyment that we, wives, feel of it. Most of them confess to me that they are disgusted by this little game, but that they are obliged to submit to it without any possible recrimination since it is their only reason for being.

I imagine that their sensitivity is atrophied because they marry too

113

young and the first act only makes them feel pain, as men are violent and fiery. They talk about it all the time, however, and do not disdain the pleasures they can procure to each others; these practices, they say, are very common in Hijaz. They question my intimate habits. Their sexual relations must be rather violent, judging by the bruises Fakria is covered with when she returns from a pleasure party with Ali Allmari. She is quite proud of them and shows them with satisfaction.

Sett Kebir keeps talking about Taif, the only place in Hijaz where there is greenery and running water. She thinks she dazzles me and makes me glimpse unknown and unimaginable lands. I tell her that at my parents' home in the country, we have a immense water road (wider than their streets) which never dries up, lined with meadows and trees ad infinitum, and that besides all, France is a large garden.

Sett Kéblr bursts out laughing, and answers me, thinking that my patriotism makes me imagine these fantastic descriptions :

– If France were as you say, it would be more beautiful than Allah's Paradise. Everybody would want to live there !

One cannot imagine how limited my conversation is with people who have never seen the most familiar objects of our everyday Western life.

One of the other topics of conversation revolves around the elegance of their toilet. They are, indeed, of an unimaginable coquetry. Each ablution is a pre-text for a change of dress. They wear a very dressy silk dress at eight o'clock in the morning, as well as a small calico dress at six o'clock in the evening. Fakria, the big favorite, appears in a new toilet three or four times a day. And she doesn't come like a person who wants to go unnoticed, but in the meantime, without a movement, her arms hanging down, her belly forward, the compliments of the assembly, who never forgets to exclaim about her beauty and elegance, just as if it was seeing her in that dress for the first time.

To brighten up these long and monotonous days, I sketched them one day with fandango, waltz and charleston steps, to the delight of these unfortunate people, who had obviously never seen anything like it. They then asked me to start over every day, and even several times a day. I became an attraction.

It then occurred to me to distract them by teaching them children's games : blindfold, ferret, rounds, farandoles, stretching exercises. Noticing an old rope lying on the ground, I jumped once : the general exhilaration was overwhelming. We call the deputy governor so that he can attend such an extraordinary thing. He swoons with laughter, with his whole harem.

When he left, the women are unleashed and utter hysterical cries, the children scream, everyone starts to run, we go up to the terrace in a frantic farandole of which I take the lead. The harem soon makes such a racket that the policemen and the soldiers of the neighboring barracks are forced to come, at the bottom of the palace, to restore order and silence.

It's a new scandal, but at least we had a good time...

The women, very agitated, then begin to beat on old empty tanakés, making a terrible racket. Then Mousny, the pretty black woman, starts dancing. She dances for hours, the women are forever chanting the measure, pushing these Arab cries, both monotonous and gloomy. Mousny, exhausted, collapses sobbing like a hunted animal; I rush to her aid and ask her what's wrong with her. She can't answer me through her tears. Sett Kebir simply says to me : "Don't worry, it's the age". I had great sympathy for Mousny, and since I had promised Soleiman that I would buy him a wife, I thought I would ask her to marry my husband. I was not very sure, moreover, that this man, petrified with pride, would agree to marry a mulatto, even the daughter of a deputy gouvernor. When I told the women about it, it took them several days to realize that it was no joke. As a young bride, I must have been jealous in their eyes. The truth is that in Hijaz today there is a trend towards the single wife, and it seemed extraordinary to them that I, as my husband's only wife, should offer him a second wife.

So I began discussing the price to be paid, and, after hours of haggling, I offered Mousny fifty pounds gold, a sum that seemed appropriate. Sett Kebir spoke to the deputy governor about it, and I, in turn, told him about it.

After long discussions, in which he always answered : "We'll see tomorrow", I thought it was a done deal, delighted to have found a derivation from Soleiman's virile ideas, when Ali Allmari quietly announced to me one morning that he had promised it to one of his cousins. I regretted Mousny, so full of charm and joie de vivre.

Behind the palace, along the sea, stood a few huts made of reed stems.

I am told that the Blacks for sale were there.

LIGHTINGS

SOLEIMAN, RETURN FROM PILGRIMAGE, COMES to me, greeting and tells me that he was unable to see the king in Mecca, to ask his permission to take me to Oneiza. As His Majesty is due to come to Djeddah shortly, all that remains is to wait. I repeat to Soleiman that he is good for nothing. In eight days, not been able to approach Ibn Saud !

– *Sabour, Sabour,* he keeps telling me. Patience. Which only exasperates me a little more. Because, like all those of his race, he is never in a hurry.

The women offer me to move to the second floor with my husband, but I tell them that I would much prefer to stay with them in the harem, if they are willing. Sett Kebir seems very touched by my attachment, but she obviously can't take the real motive into account. She takes advantage of this to tease me about my lack of enthusiasm for marital duty. Soleiman, vexed, did not spend any nights at the Deputy Governor's, and I never knew exactly where he slept. He came to greet me every morning and went up the stairs shouting "Zeinab" after a slave had clapped his hands. For the first time, he gave up the name "Madam". I then went down to the second floor where we talked about our travel plans. He regularly gave me a little lesson on what I should not do and not say to the harem, and he seemed to claim marital authority which I tried to limit. I felt, moreover, that he was lying to me perpetually. Thus, he told me one day that he had met ten pilgrims from Palmyra, one of whom was the sister of Ahmed, my cook. I begged him to bring her to me so that I could give her a message for my family. As he could never let me see her, I concluded that his story was false.

He also told me that he had found the man in Mecca to whom we had entrusted the one hundred gold pounds to take them to Oneiza. So I asked him to give me back the money, but he replied :

– I told him to continue on Oneiza, so that we would find that money when we arrived.

A new lie, since he had returned with debts from the pilgrimage. He had even had to borrow from our friend the Hindu.

Finally, he told me one day that he had arranged with a caravan to cross the desert.

The king being in Djeddah, the whole city is decked out with flags, and banners in the Nedjian colors, green and white, put cheerfulness in this severe city.

The cannon thunders every day.

I send Soleiman to see the sovereign, making him put on his most beautiful green and gold "naouls" and giving him a new kéfié.

Unsure of him, I decide at the same time, but without him knowing it, to go on my side and I leave, not without difficulty, by car, accompanied by Lotfi, a twelve year old boy and son of Sett Kébir who recommended him to take great care of me...

The palace where the king lives belongs to Soleiman Abdallah, Ibn Saud's Minister of Finance and, by the way, cousin of my esteemed husband Soleiman. It is a vast blue construction, completely isolated in the middle of the sands, on the deeply rutted road leading to Mecca.

On either side of the entrance, a long line of Blacks stands guard. Their red dresses are gold brocaded and lined with purple, at the sleeves and at the bottom.

They are straight, imposing, uniformly very tall.

Their weapons are gigantic silver sabres, which curved point rests on the ground and which hilt comes to their chest.

All the color, all the allure of this HeJazian royalty is in this polychrome vision.

Certainly no woman has ever been seen coming here alone, and a swarm of men rush in on me when they see me. Lotfi, moved, stays in the car that has been stopped at a certain distance. I make known to those around me with great politeness my desire to speak to the king or one of his ministers. The "prefect" is called Aboued Taa, kaimacam of Djeddah. He arrives. He is a very skinny Arab, with a nose like a toucan's beak, who reminds one of some mummies in the Cairo museum. He leads me into a living room. There, a man from Syria asks me in very good French the purpose of the audience I am seeking. There, the Minister of Foreign Affairs arrives. His name is Fouad Hamza. I explain to him that having married a Nedjian, it is without any reason that   I was arrested in Djeddah. So I came to ask the monarch's permission to follow my husband to his family in Oneiza, passing through Mecca and Medina.

The Minister goes out to transmit this request.

There is little time left and he comes back to tell me that His Majesty is extremely busy at the moment. But Soleiman only has to present my request himself. The king will receive it at once.

Unfortunately, I know the laziness of Soleiman, as well as the detours of this spirit filled with ulterior motives. I therefore confirm that I would like to speak to the king myself in order to know precisely the limits of what he authorizes and forbids.

Fouad Hamza assures me that everything will be explained properly to Soleiman... and that there will be no chance of error. Ibn

Saud has already had all his hearings taken today, he cannot receive me. I understand it since he has just arrived, but I keep on asking for an appointment for later. Fouad Hamza, without being impatient, but to finish, tells me that the muslim law is opposed to the king seeing a woman besides his wives.

I expressed the hope that he would make an exception for me, a stranger :

– You are a muslim, and you have stopped being a foreigner, the minister said with a sharp gesture.

This time the audience was well over, I left the palace with regret. As I left, I glanced admiringly at the astonishing guard, gold, scarlet and violet.

Soleiman, whom I had thought to find at the palace or on the road, had remained untraceable. I then hoped that he would be at home, and my desire was to send him urgently to see the king. I couldn't find him anywhere, and no one knew where he had gone. During his morning visit the next day, he lied to me and told me that Ibn Saud had not been able to receive him : "Joker, you didn't go there. Fouad Hamza had you searched uselessly. Go now. His glorious Majesty awaits you". He leaves.

At eleven o'clock, M... calls me to invite me for lunch. He did not want a French woman to pass through Djeddah without being received at the House of France. I accept, as you can easily guess, and I tell Sett Kebir that I am leaving for the consulate.

– You are not ashamed ! she exclaims, to see "nosranis" christians like this over and over again. How modest you are, to dare to speak freely to men! If you don't change, you will never become a good and true muslim.

I reply :

– I will be muslim like the women of Turkey and Egypt, which I know very well, and which are far more emancipated than I am here.

She is silent. I put on my veil and my beautiful golden belt, found in the souk of Djeddah, then I leave the harem, followed by my slaves : Ahmed is in a tan color dress and Choukry in peppermint green. Lunch is very lively. There are French people from North Africa who have come for the pilgrimage.

Hamdi bey, the vice-consul, a man of great pres- tance, does the honors. It is an old cadi, of the Algiers department. He is decorated with the Legion of Honor. I have an extraordinary pleasure in this atmosphere : plates, cutlery, butlers, French food, champagne... It is necessary to have lived as I lived since my sequestration to enjoy all this in its fullness.

While I let myself go to the joy of finding myself in this atmosphere, Mr. M... invites me for lunch tomorrow, Easter day, on one of the French boats that are in a harbor. Reason tells me to refuse. But prudence, at this moment, is silent in my happy soul and I accept. Of course, when I return and announce this news, dismay reigns among the women.

Sett Kebir gives me in vain the moral, "her moral". All she gets from me is that Lotfi will ac- company me.

I have a good sense that he will come to watch me, to see how I stand with the "nosranis".

Everything seems to be going very well on this Easter day. There are great people on the boat I arrive on, with the members of the French delegation, the minister of Iraq and the minister of Persia, found in the launch that brings me there.

Lunch is very cheerful, the food and the wine are excellent : truffled foie gras and champagne are on the menu. The conversation is lively, particularly brilliant, but unfortunately my pleasure of chatting in French makes me forget the danger of speaking too freely.

The minister of Persia keeps telling me that I must be more careful in my words. As I tell him that I don't care, he replies to me straightforwardly :

– If you are not afraid for yourself, you could at least worry about those around you.

He's worried that I might compromise Ali Allmari. Of course, he believes in the presence of spies everywhere.

After lunch, everyone starts playing bridge and poker. I take the opportunity to walk on the deck. The sea is blue, of a blue unknown in our countries... The surface of the water is so calm that one would hardly be surprised to see people walking on it.

A gramophone plays foxtrot, probably the latest hits from Paris. This contact of civilization is pleasant for me and I dance a little. I feel like I'm at a costume ball, on some yacht on the Riviera, especially because of my astonishing costume, which is neither completely Arab, nor Hindu, nor obviously Parisian. But I can see the conspiratorial Arabs arriving on board. They seem to come for a courtesy visit.

My dancer then whispers to me :

– They are spies. Boats in harbor, against the international custom, are not recognized as foreign territory. The king may, at his discretion, exercise surveillance, and his permission is required to anchor or sail.

Lotfi, distraught among these Europeans, at once severe and friendly, seductive and disdainful, had to leave. I find it difficult to make him admit that customs and politeness demand my presence here until the departure of the consul, by whom I was brought on this boat. We leave the ship at about five o'clock. But it is to go and have a "whisky and soda" on an English ship. The armchairs there have a truly British comfort. The dance music is catchy, the day ends well.

We return to the harem at eight o'clock ! Mr. M... accompanies me there, given the late hour in this country.

Through the "moucharabiehs" on the third floor, the women watched me with an ardent curiosity. Sett Kebir ran to ask me who was accompanying me. I simply say

– He is the French consul.

But these women from the East understand nothing about our life. She saw Mr. M... get up in the car, shake my hand, leave his helmet, bow. These signs of deference seem inexplicable to her. And she responds with an amusing irony :

– Are you crazy ? Is a consul going to bother for a simple woman like you !

But they are not at the end of their surprises. A word from Mr. M... was brought to me by a slave. He tells me that the planned hunting trip on the English ship, for the next day, is handed over. On the other hand, at dawn, a phone call from Mr. M..'s son puts the business back on its feet. He tells me that a car is coming to pick me up. Amazement, bewilderment filled with the smell of the harem. In this monotonous, oppressive and sad existence, where life is a kind of perpetual drowsiness, I bring the revolution. I drive along the sea.

It's a strange sight to see such a flat and clean expanse. We drive for an hour without any change in the landscape, as if we had stayed in the same place. Our guns seem to be a joke, not the slightest trace of game. A naked immensity, always more naked. Only a few forgotten camel droppings (because the Arabs carefully collect them to make fire) testify to the passage of an animal life. Renouncing necessarily the gazelles, I propose a bath, in this sea so attractive, doubly attractive for me, after the ablutions of the harem, which are rather a pain than a delight. The heat is scorching.

What a delightful bath !

I come back with a kind of certainty, this time, that one can, in truth, accommodate oneself to the harems... Provided that one leaves them often...

Mr. M...'s son comes to pick me up the next day to offer me to go swimming again. We set off again by car on the immensity of the plain. We decided not to go too far, the king's brother coming for lunch at Ali Allmari's house. They want me to be at the harem, in case he has me asked, something exceptional for a woman and which proves how well the officials abandoned their prejudices for me.

After about 40 kilometers, the car stops dead, and our driver tells us quietly that it's a gas shortage. We are in the middle of the desert, on the horizon only a blue patch, which completes the golden part of the sand. We do not even see the sea anymore. Mr. M...'s son and I, after a brief conciliation, decide to send the driver to Djeddah to get gas. In the meantime, we go swimming in the sea, but we still have to find it...

We set off on an adventure, relying on our sense of direction. We walk for hours under a scorching sun, the throat so dry that I can't even swallow without pain. We protect ourselves from sunstroke by instituting, every five minutes, a shift change system, for the wearing of M's son colonial helmet.

Still nothing on the horizon. Suddenly, a huge palm grove in shades of blue appears on the edge of a shimmering lake. We do not feel any more thirst so much we are preoccupied to arrive at this water as quickly as possible. Mirage... Soon nothing remains but the arid sand and the sky. Entire oases, rivers, lakes, are born and die before our eyes.

We walk in the midst of this desolation, in what we believe to be the direction of the sea, underpinned by this hallucinating desire to drink, see or hear water.

Finally a blue line appears in the distance, we are taken by a horrible anguish at the idea of a new illusion. Ten minutes, the stingray appears blue all the time, twenty minutes, the stingray has become a lake, and we see the beach. A beach on which we can walk, without it slipping away under our feet in a fantastic mystification.

We find a tiny triangular tent, with a Bedouin fisherman and his son. We hurry towards them to ask for water. They take out of an old tanaké an old yellowish liquid, full of sand and oil, which they offer us in a rusty sardine can. I moisten my tongue, my throat, that's all I wanted. I can barely feel the foul taste of it, so great is the enjoyment of this liquid in the dried gullet. Besides, I prefer sea water, despite the protests of M. son. We put ourselves out of sight of these people, since my bath is forbidden by Islam. The sand is so hot that you can't set foot in it without getting horribly burned, and I run to soak myself in this divine sin.

At two hundred meters, the enormous ray that the waves make when breaking on the coral banks creates a natural lagoon between the reefs and the beach. This delimits the pool where we are safe from sharks.

The water is wonderfully transparent. Soon the multicolored carpet at the bottom has no more secrets for us. We play with the sponges we come in contact with. We make a speed race on huge pearly shells, which makes us look like some extra from a Casino de Paris magazine. We end this afternoon of vacation with an interminable sunbath. Then the fearsome walk starts again in the opposite direction, the same mirages come back, the reverberation is so strong that we can see the aerial undulations of the burning atmosphere. We finally find the car, still without driver. We sit on the cushions, resigned. After an hour, we see a car on the horizon in a cloud of yellow sand. Is it a mirage or a reality ? The vision becomes clearer and it is a car loaded with Bedouins among whom is our driver.

HOPE

WE RETURN TO DJEDDAH EXHAUSTED, I AM burning from the fever caused by horrible sunburns, forming a belt on my hips, between the end of my little indoor vest and the beginning of my pants. Sett Kebir looks at me, dismayed at the punishment that Allah has inflicted on me for violating his sacred precepts once again.

On my return to the harem, Soleiman, who had been missing for two days, immediately lectures me.

– The king, he said to me, called me to the palace to reproach me for your conduct. He found out that you went dancing on the boats of the "nosranis" and finds that these freedoms are unworthy of a good Muslim woman.

I retaliate bitterly

– All you had to do was answer that it's his fault, that it's up to him to stop all these scandals by quickly giving me permission to leave, instead of holding me prisoner here.

However, Soleiman's distress is acute. I become conciliatory, and I promise to my husband, because I guess he speaks in our interest, not to do it again. I want to succeed.

Is there in the world an agglomeration of human beings without espionage or gossip ?

No, probably not, since that very evening the Deputy Chief of Police came to question me in due form. I answer as best as I can.

When I tell him that I have spent ten years of my life in boarding school, from five to fifteen years old, he doesn't understand, because in two years of class, the Nedjian instruction is complete. So what have I been able to do in so much time ?

He wants to know if I am an architect or a doctor, what are my diplomas and patents, since I have studied so much.

Then it is the question that haunts all the heads of the East :

– Why did you become a Muslim ?

– I believe that this religion leads to the truth. He, then, has an astonishing word.

– Only that ? He says..." Bus".

There is, of course, an abyss, abysses between our two brains. Moreover, my Arabic is miserable and we understand each other only halfway. I ask him for an interpreter who knows my language in order to better understand me. He is looking for this interpreter, but in Djeddah there are perhaps four people who speak French. And they are high-ranking civil servants, who cannot be disturbed, so he comes back empty-handed, this deputy director of the police. I had to meet him again soon and under what tragic circumstances !

The next day, I think I see the end of my wait coming, and I imagine, perhaps naively, that things will work out on their own. I have waited long enough, put up with vexations and inconveniences. I believe that this is the end of the tunnel.

Not, moreover, that I can sincerely believe that everything will be rosy to reach Oneiza, cross this terrible desert of Hofouf and reach the Persian Gulf.

But the idle waiting and the prospect of difficulties is worse than the difficulties themselves.

Soleiman comes to teach me that finally the king gives us the authorization to go to Oneiza. We will be able to pass by Medina. But, to visit Mecca, it is necessary that a council of *ulemas (1)* decides if it considers it suitable. It would be perfect if Soleiman hadn't lied to me so much that I now find it hard to believe him.

However, I promised not to go out anymore. But why not ask my friends from the consulate to come and have tea at Ali Allmari's house ?

And I phone to formulate this invitation.

On that, Mr. M... comes to see me. He is worried about my initiative. The idea of entering a Hajjazi interior gives him some concern and he leaves as soon as possible, without even crossing the threshold of the large door of the hall.

The next day, Mr. M...'s son brought back my watchband, left at the consulate.

I ask him to get me some ink and stationery, because in this haphazard and difficult existence I have not been able to write to my family, and I have to do it at last. He brings me, shortly afterwards, something to write with.

But every word I say, every desire I formulate, every gesture now shakes the whole harem. Certainly I am tolerated a lot of things; however, the last visit of the evening makes the cup overflow...

It's M...'s son again. He ignores almost all Muslim customs. So he does not think he is doing wrong by simply saying hello, in the Western way, to the Deputy governor, without asking him, as the rites of Arab courtesy require, and to see me and why he is making this request.

(I) *Uléma, great religious leader.*

As soon as he left, Ali Allmari, in a fit of rage, arrived and shouted that I was defiling his house by constantly receiving "nosranis".

I see that nothing can calm him down, and while he throws his curses like an inspired prophet, I cut him off :

– Don't make so much noise, I will leave your house tomorrow.

Sett Kebir is in consternation. But I make her understand that Ali Allmari has seriously outraged me. The evening goes gloomily. The women, crouching around the poor lamp, seem like wax figures, or those replicas of Arab life that were one of the glories of the Colonial Exhibition.

I finish embroidering the initials of a jumpsuit promised to Fakria and a hemmed handkerchief, with small butterflies in color for Moussny, because my sewing work had conquered the harem. I seem sad, but I am delighted with the incident that allows me to escape from this damned confinement. I regret leaving some women who were very kind to me. I have a real affection for Sett Kebir.

I lie for the last time on the floor of this very hospitable house and dream of my next trip.

The king, it seems, has allowed me to act with more freedom once in the interior of the lands, during my trip, and even according to my European customs. But is this true ? It is too good...

At dawn, I prepare myself for a challenging start. Sett Kébir sees me as unshakeable. She cries and indicates me, in the souks, a room that must suit me. Around nine o'clock, it is the last breakfast. It is like coming out of a funeral. We only talk about eternal friendships and, up to those who love me the least, all of them are full of attention. Sett Kebir dreams of seeing me again in Basra; Fakria alone remains silent. This tells me that Ali Allmari has told her not to try to hold me back any longer.

I eat the famous black honey from Medina which was my main

and best food here. I don't have enough oaths of affection for everyone.

Suddenly, I hear Soleiman calling me in the street. He appears, looking unhappy, and shouts :

– Pack your bags, we're leaving.

– That is good. I had decided to leave this morning.

He asks, exasperated :

– And where do you want to go ?

– Sett Kébir knows a room very well in the souks.

– I don't need advice from anyone, let alone Sett Kebir, he shouts like a deaf man. You're going to come to my house, to my home. Pack our bags right now and leave without saying goodbye.

I run upstairs to pack our things. Fifteen minutes later, I go back downstairs. I had to kiss all the women several times, promising Sett Kebir to come and see her every day.

But when I went down to the hall, I no longer see Soleiman. I question the slaves. He has gone to look for a house, they answer me.

– Looking for a house, but didn't he say he was going to take me to his ?

I hurriedly went back upstairs to ask Sett Kebir for a slave to take me to the room she told me about. This good friend fears that I will be locked up and that we will not be able to see each other again, she will try to have me followed, to know what I am becoming, but, if I am at the place she tells me, we will surely be able to see each other or at least communicate.

We leave for the souks. Alas ! everything is rented. Feeling more and more emancipated, I send the slave back and go to the consulate to ask if someone knows a hotel. I'm told that one has just opened, not far away.

The consul's son kindly offers to accompany me. But an Arab woman in the street, with a European man, is enough to make headlines. Also are we covered with a mute reprobation by a hundred angry glances.

The hotel consists of a series of rooms overlooking a central hall. Each room has several beds, and I occupy the smallest one which has only three beds.

But there are no toiletries, the large beds in which I haven't slept for more than a month tempt me and seem to me the height of luxury.

However, I wouldn't want to retain this room if Soleiman combined something else. I don't know what to do. I go back to Ali Allmari's house, where he was never seen again.

What happened, since he had come to tell me to pack immediately and follow him ? Here is the enigma...

Certainly, the Deputy Governor would be delighted to receive me again, but I cannot bring myself to ask for it after the scene of the day before. I decide that I will stay at my new home. Everyone is invited to tell Soleiman where I am when they see him again. A maid then picks up my suitcases and brings them to the hotel. But after barely an hour there, this loneliness depresses and crushes me. I'm going out.

Here I am outside. I reach the seaside. My gait is awkward because of the double black veil, and I have to watch the ground at my feet because of the interval that my breathing provokes by spreading the veil... But I am not unhappy, I even taste a new quality of my freedom. It is precious to me, after the forced confinement of the last weeks.

However, I wonder what the unexplainable disappearance of

Soleiman means, and what it hides for the future ?

I get home at around six o'clock. Lotfi and a slave come to bring me bamias, my favorite dish. This proof of affection and concern from Sett Kebir touches and comforts me.

And we are still talking about Soleiman, who has been missing since the morning, to everyone's astonishment. I fear the night. A muslim woman should never sleep alone. The hotel guests looked at me with an unpleasant insistence. The boss knocks constantly at my door without a shadow of reason.

We must fear everything, from lust to fanaticism. Here he is again, this obsequious hotelier

– I come to see how you are ?

"How long have you been married ?"

"Are you hungry ? Here are some cakes". Angry, I beg them to leave me in peace.

This furnished house was created solely for the convenience of pilgrims. It has moreover a kind of official character. Perhaps I will be there, all things considered, better than I thought.

ARREST

I AM NOT AFRAID AT DAY, BUT IT HAPPENS to me, in the loneliness of the night, to have atrocious anxieties and, this, since i was a child. I then have cold sweats and I drag myself into abominable nightmares. Neither reasoning nor willpower have ever been able to overcome this kind of terror that immobilizes me in a kind of haunted paralysis.

So I waited that night without joy and watched out for all the noises outside. The windows were without moucharabiehs, but with iron grills I could watch what was going on in the street, and even listen... That's why, hearing footsteps, I came to look. I recognized M...'s son. He would talk in a low voice to check up on me and ask about Soleiman. We converse for a while through the bars. I tell him about my night terrors, he offers to spend the evening with me, waiting for Soleiman. I accept, like an independent French woman, who cares little about what people will say.

But, i can feel that the anguish is back.

However the act is serious, because I am muslim. With what happened today, my escape, especially from Ali Allmari, everything would seem a terrible premeditation of the act of which I would be accused if we were caught together. But everything is asleep, let's go !

M...'s son manages to sneak into my house without being seen by the night watchmen. Or did he give them a "bakshich"? We start chatting quietly. Time passes. We discuss how to make it go unnoticed. He finds the situation amusing, he even laughs when someone knock on the door.

Silence, one moment.

One more knock on my door.

I ask nervously :

– Who's there ?

The slaves of the hotel shout together :

– Come quickly, you are asked on the phone.

I reassure myself. All that is however very strange, and I question :

– At this hour, who can ask me ?

– Open, open fast.

– No, I wouldn't open like this in the middle of the night for anything in the world.

In my opinion, Mr. M...'s son was seen entering here and they set a trap for me.

They move away, then they come back :

– Come quickly, Soleiman is very sick. I'm being mocked ! I retaliate :

– How, Soleiman is sick ? But I saw him this morning and he was fine. I won't open.

This time, they keep quiet. I am worried. Then my horror increases and takes shape. It is absolutely necessary to get this Frenchman out before dawn, because otherwise...

We discuss possible escapes : can the bars of the window be broken ? Or, disguised as an Arab woman, would he be able to walk away without being recognized ?

Suddenly, we hear the sound of the telephone again and a voice repeats over there :

– Very sick, half dead, but Zeinab does not want to open.

This time I get a hit. I no longer think it is a trick to get me to open up and fear a real misfortune. I have to go to the phone. But what am I going to do, during this time, of this cumbersome host, whose mere presence puts us in a risk of death ?

I am going to hide him under the bed.

It's done. Then, calmly, in an attitude that I would like to be natural, without betraying my emotion by a slow or nervously fast gait, I open the door and go out. My heart beats terribly. My throat is tight. I reach the receiver. I take it for a moment. Then I hear Ali Allmari's voice. He confirms to me that Soleiman is at his worst. He accuses me of having poisoned him by making him take an allegedly purgative powder.

I reply : "It is true that I gave my husband several days ago some "kalmine" pills and a purgative. But these are the same products that I gave to the women of the harem. And there were no troubles with them.

– When did you give him this ?

– Eight days ago. Since then, I haven't made him take anything.

Silence.

Everything is going wrong in my business. I decide to take refuge at the French consulate. I quickly hang up, and then I shout to the slaves to immediately pull the locks of the front door. At the same time, I run to my room to warn young M... that there is only one thing left to do, to escape any way we can.

I hastily take my veil, my cape, in which I become entangled. Quickly... quickly...

It is already too late. In the generally absolute silence at this hour, a sound of steel tinkles with hurried steps. Bayonet rattling, dogs barking.

They are soldiers, who make the calm night of Djeddah resound.

I see these armed men in the gap, just as we are about to go out into the street. I rush to my room, I close the door. Do they come to execute me ? I push Mr. M...'s son under the bed. At the same moment, rifle butts shake my door. It is necessary at all costs to avoid revealing the presence of the visitor in my room, otherwise our death is certain. A man found in the company of a woman : in Hijaz, such a fact is enough to make the crime of adultery be considered flagrant, and no judgment is required for the execution of the death penalty, which can be carried out on the spot. The whole mentality of the Arabs can be understood by the simple fact that, in their minds, a man cannot even think of seeing a woman for any reason other than carnal pleasures.

One can imagine my shock. What to do ? Above all, to not open, and I tell them that a woman does not open her door at night, and I persist until the moment when it is demolished by the butts of rifles and bayonets.

So I open the door and, looking almost astonished, I find myself in front of a tall man with a hard mask, a wild and fierce expression, black teeth in a very tanned face. Don't move. His gaze stares at me with oppressive tenacity. He has a diabolical air, immense in his black abbey and his white kéfié, which makes his figure even more frightening. However, he is perfectly correct and introduces himself : "moudir cherta", police director. Saïd Bey.

Arabic politeness is never at fault.

Behind him, in the shadows, glittering weapons. He is surrounded by a whole escort of policemen and soldiers.

I beg Saïd Bey to take me to Soleiman, who in front of me will never say that I gave him poison. I cling to his arm and try with all possible energy to drag him to the hospital where Soleiman is dying; but Saïd Bey just asks me the same questions as Ali Allmari. Even though I maintain that I haven't given anything to Soleiman for eight days, I am arrested.

Just as I'm about to be taken away, the telephone rings : it is the Emir of Djeddah, who gives the order that I am allowed to finish the night at the hotel, and that they put me in prison only in the morning.

I breathe better, I have hope again to be able to escape with Mr. M...'s. son. But, of course, I had counted without the director of police. He sits on a chair behind my door, while the soldiers, armed, stand guard in the corridor and in front of my windows.

It's all over, I'm a prisoner...

THE PRISON

I BEND UNDER THE BED TO CALL SOFTLY M...'s son. But my voice doesn't come out. My mouth is as dry as an oven and my tongue sticks to the palate. With my finger, I peel it off. Certainly, in front of the danger, we multiply. I answered with ease. Better still, I found in my memory Arabic words that are not part of my customary vocabulary, which is rather limited. Peril gives vigor and I faced it. But nothing is over and the next few hours are frightening. Mr. M...'s son makes me the amazing proposal to go out. He brandishes an Arab dagger and mimes offensive gestures. I find it hard to calm him down and prove to him that, if he succeeds at best in killing two or three men, and they are all used to hand-to-hand combat, there will be twenty or thirty left to kill us.

Mr. M...'s son then said to me kindly : "Rest while I watch, tomorrow you will need all your strength".

It is the only thing to do indeed. We lie down side by side, very softly and fully dressed, on the same bed, to be able to converse with the minimum of noise. The wake begins, agonizing.

My companion tells me that the week before, the governor of Medina tied a man guilty of adultery to the tail of a horse with his arms. It goes without saying that the unfortunate man was horribly mutilated.

At two o'clock the call of the muezzin is accompanied by sounds of weapons in our corridor. The police prays too. In front of my windows, soldiers come and go, and in the hall conversations continue in a low voice. Probably the police chiefs are having coffee or playing dice.

Through a screened skylight, the guards who occupy the room next door dive into my room. But they can't see us in the dark and under the mosquito net. Every time I speak, I pull Mr. M...'s son's head out by his hair and whisper, with my mouth applied to his ear.

The dawn finally comes. Saïd Bey finds that the moment of politeness has passed. Through the door he calls me. I half-open the door and slip my terrified head into the corridor.

He shouts :

– Prepare yourself. I'm taking you.

I say feverishly :

– So be it. Let's go and see Soleiman and you'll see that he will not accuse me.

– Later, now you only have to follow me.

No discussion, he is stubborn and hard as a rock.

I push back the door and arrange my veil. I arrange also my suitcase. My comrade reproaches me for not having presented him to the chief of police. I smile in spite of myself as if it was time for introductions when the worst is about to happen.

No one knows he's there. If, however, I could accustom Saïd Bey to his presence and act in such a way that he finds it normal... Then he will be able to appear in the eyes of the guard without provoking, at least I hope, the reactions of anger that would end up in our common lynching.

I open the door and I beckon Saïd Bey. Two or three faithful policemen follow him. I push them away, making them understand that I want to talk one-on-one with their chief. As soon as he enters, as naturally as possible, I point out my companion who looks wildly scowling. He barely seems to be able to hold his ground. He forgets that, in such a situation, the help of diplomacy is our only chance of salvation.

– "Shouf" ! Look...

And Saïd Bey looks, his eyes wide-open, he stares at Mr. M...'s son. A cruel grin uncovers his teeth as black as his skin, the expression of his face hardens again, his hatred, his anger, his stupor are intense. His body tensed, his head stretched forward, he articulates in jerks : "Min... Min ? Who's that ? Who is this man ? What is he doing in your room ?"

– He is the son of the Delegate of France, he came to spend the evening with me. I was scared alone and he could not leave since you were there.

No answer, but the face becomes more and more ferocious... and little by little, behind him, the door is pushed open. A few policemen come in, I want to send them again, but Saïd Bey beckons me to let them come. The faces are expressive, wild. However, the chief does not move, and all, following his example, control themselves. Silence, contempt, more tragic than insults or blows. Through the door, in the half-light of the dawning day, the silvery net of bayonets shines.

I'm interpreting, because Saïd Bey asks :

– Does he know me ?

Dogged, Mr. M...'s son answers : "No".

Saïd Bey articulates :

– I know him, does he ride a horse ?

M... son : "Yes".

– He rode the police director's horse, mine, and, since I know him, I know he has a diplomatic passport. He is free.

My comrade doesn't move, I want to push him, it's an unexpected opportunity to be able to warn the consulate.

– I don't want to leave you alone, he insists gently. God knows where they will take you and what they will do with you.

– Of course, but there is nothing you can do about it. My only hope of salvation is Mr. your father, please go quickly and tell him everything, I beg you.

Then I revolt against the mudir cherta who wants to seize me and I cry out :

– Where are you going to take me ? What are you going to do ? I don't want to go with you, I'm afraid !

With his frightening smile and the unalterable politeness of the Oriental, he answers : "Don't be afraid with me, you are my sister !"(sic).

What resistance to this strong softness ? This man, convinced of my guilt, convinced of my next execution, calls me : "My sister" !

I smile and want to be up to a situation with no way out, I put my hand on his arm and add :

– I trust you, I follow you.

The policemen stuff the suitcases with me (I have Soleiman's and mine), pack everything with their fists or their heels, the wall of weapons opens up.

I cross the hall, head high, go down the stairs and I don't realize what's going on until I'm in a car. Saïd Bey is next to me. Next to the driver, on the footboards, bunches of soldiers and policemen stand up, armed to the teeth.

The car starts, we drive along the legation of Iraq, the legation of France... can I escape, can I jump out of the auto ? But, assuming I don't break a leg when I fall, I would immediately be shot by these armed people.

Besides, it is so early that the doors are still closed and I would have to enter in a hurry to succeed. Besides, it's over, the French consulate is no longer in front of me, the car is stopped in front of a small white house, overhanging, supported in the Red Sea by a few pilotis. The second floor is surrounded by a balcony that gives it the unexpected aspect of a small villa.

The guard immediately surrounds me as I cross the threshold of the prison. I pass first, the soldiers stand at attention when I reach the first balcony terrace. A sentry then signals me to continue further. I climb a staircase, a real ladder, to reach a large room, blinding with sun and light. No moucharabieh diminishes the day. This clarity gives me a bitter feeling of freedom and life as a gem of the last days of the harem. And yet, this time I am a prisoner for good.

Saïd bey comes forward, then, solemnly, sits behind his desk. He shows me, with a gesture, the window on the sea where he advises me to breathe: "Awa koyes", the good wind.

I use it to my advantage. Sitting on the ledge, I take a deep breath of salty air. Don't I have to stock up on forces for the struggle I'm going to have to endure ?

For almost an hour, everyone seems to have forgotten my presence. I count the time it takes for the sea undulations to die, I look off into the distance. There are ships in harbour and I think about whether I can swim to them. But it is a vain dream. They are three, four, six kilometers away... And, in truth, I'm rambling on and on, because how far would the sharks let me go ?

But Mr. M...'s son was released. He returned to the Consulate and his father is coming. All my hope rests on him.

Then I think of my little red notebook, which contains all my impressions and thoughts about each one. It is the summary of my journey. I ask to leave for a short moment. I'm allowed to, but two sentinels accompany me and supervise me. I almost forgot that I am arrested. It reminds me of my situation.

Once alone, however, I slip the little red notebook held by my belt onto my belly.

Once again unimaginable agitation fills the police station. The comings and goings of the soldiers are accompanied by the din that in any country is strictly military : the clattering of sticks, foot calls, heel slapping, repeated every time the police director enters or leaves.

The phone rings relentlessly. It must be the hospital, the doctors, the people at Soleiman's bedside.

I hear interspersed sentences

– Are you coming ?

– Yes, she is here.

– Her suitcase was seized.

– She denies the crime.

Now it's car squeaks coming up from outside, with many voices and resonant horns. They climb up the stairs and three men enter the room where I am.

All three are tall, well-groomed, elegant, they have thin skin and a face framed by black curls. One of them is astonishing, with his complexion too pale, his nose pinched, his eyes glassy at the top of his head. The instinct that rarely deceives me tells me that this is a fearsome enemy. They are doctors. They get together with Jaber

Effendi, deputy director of the police, and start whispering away from me, occasionally giving me menacing glances.

I listen to them and understand that Soleiman would get better. New car noise and renewed tumult in the staircase.

Here is the moudir cherta himself.

He is calm and impassive. When he comes in, everyone rushes towards him. And I do the same and hold on to his arm and shake it so that he answers me.

– Have you seen Soleiman ?

Everyone is amazed at my audacity. They look at me with mixed horror and respect.

Moudir cherta is the great chief of police.

He agrees to answer me :

– Yes, I saw him. He even threw up in front of me.

And he mimics nausea.

– Why don't you take me to see him ?

– He has a tired head and fever.

– Does he always say that I was the one who poisoned him ?

– Yes, he still accuses you.

– So he's very angry with me ?

– No, he speaks very well of you.

I don't understand anything about it. Doctors listen with gawping ears, looking fierce, ready to punish my impudence. One of them comes forward and looks me straight in the eye, and says :

– Soleiman accuses you of poisoning him. In addition, three roommates certify having seen him take, at around ten o'clock in the evening, a red powder diluted in water. When these three Arabs asked him what he had taken, he replied : "Zeinab gave me this to purge me".

– Without hesitation, I answer : it's not true. I'm sure Soleiman never said that.

– As a joke, Soleiman also added :

"Maybe Zeinab loves another man and she gives me this to set herself free".

It's too stupid and I question, indignant :

– Did the witnesses say this before or after my arrest ?

– Why this ?

– Because they certainly invented it afterwards. If he had been afraid of something, he obviously wouldn't have been drinking. He is suspicious of everything in the world. Now, with the help of imagination, witnesses will affirm as true everything that one want them to say.

One, doctor steps forward :

– A very small pill was found near his bed. He says he swal-

lowed a similar one. He got it from you. Tell us what it is.

I shrug my shoulders, I know that none of this is true. Soleiman would not have taken drugs given by others, and eight days ago I gave him a kalmine pill and purgative powder bought in Suez for the headache.

This is not what could have poisoned him. But the doctors saw my suitcase

– Those are your belongings ?

– Yes !

They throw themselves on it. There is certainly the proof of my crime. They rush about, ripping off objects from each others hands.

Finally, one of them brandishes a box of cocoa.

— The brown powder that was intended for Soleiman. Here it is.

I explain to them, as I can, that it is a very concentrated food, which is diluted in milk or hot water and which I took with me when I crossed the desert.

I want to eat it in front of them, to prove it's innocent, but they take the box away from me.

Now they ask me about my face powder. I shake the puff under their noses as a demonstration.

The red lipstick, blush, and even nail polish must also be explained. They are flabbergasted by the use of all these products.

Saïd bey looks at me haughtily and says with contempt :

— Everything for the face...

Finally, we get our hands on a hundred Kalmine pills, and here is the laxative powder. They are greeted with triumphant, fierce and exalted shouts of triumph.

I continue my explanations which, in other cir- constancies, would be comical, but I must not forget that I am playing with my life.

I take the purgative and hit my stomach screaming :

— "Botné nédif" (clean belly).

It is more ungrateful to provide a valid explanation of the effects of Kalmin. I try to explain, by making cabalistic signs on my head, that it calms the migraine.

They're not convinced, all I tell them seems suspicious to them.

But the content of the pills may be the so-called red powder that poisoned Soleiman ? I open a pill. The powder is indeed pale pink. Amazement. I ask for water. Who knows if the powder doesn't get darker once dissolved ?

The chief asks the chaouich (police officer) to bring a coffee cup with a few drops of water.

The color is accentuated.

I feel so eager to prove my innocence that I would do anything for it. And, in order to prove the safety of Kalmine, I will swallow the contents of the cup.

I'm not prompt enough. Three terrified hands are holding me back, and the whole thing is carefully thrown into the sea.

To persuade these men filled with doubt and suspicion, I would like to take everything together, the cocoa, the pills, the power... But they fear accidents and suicide. Finally, a chaouich, with laughable precautions, as if they were dangerous explosives, takes away all my cosmetics, my remedies and my food...

The search of my suitcase continues. But the pale doctor watches me and pushes me around. He imagines that I want to hide something.

I step back and insult him : nasty, stupid, you don't understand anything. I wanted to make your job easier and make you understand all these things that are unknown to you.

As I'm being groped to see if I'm not hiding anything, my red notebook was seized. I tear out two little talismans that I always carry on my heart and I throw them on the ground in spite, in powerlessness, crying out : "It's for (bart) luck, I don't want it anymore".

These worthy men get down on all fours to pick up these gris-gris, while I burst out with a nervous laugh at the thought of the reactions provoked by the cabalistic signs that cover the parchment. After finally turning my incomprehensible good-luck charms upside down, they pretend to believe the explanations I give them.

INTERROGATORY

THEN IT'S THE TURN OF MY PAPERS, A FEW letters that might seem compromising, a very good map of Arabia, a letter written for my son, a few books; each sheet is examined as if it were a sensational document, establishing my guilt.

Saïd bey beckons me to sit down in front of him, while he stares at me, his teeth clenched, straddling a chair in front of me. He then gradually imparts a frenzied back and forth movement to his legs. He looks like an epileptic. I look at him bewildered, while, sweating and shouting, he repeats :

– "Haki saï ! " Speak true... Speak true.

– I always tell the truth, all the Arabs of Syria know it, ask Soleiman instead. He will tell you that I never lie.

– Haki saï. Speak true... Speak true... You gave him poison yesterday morning, when he came to see you at the harem, we saw you...

– Everybody lies, they couldn't see me because I didn't give anything. I was alone with him, it only lasted two minutes and we didn't even touch our hands.

Where could I have hidden poison in the women's indoor suit, bare feet, bare arms ?

– Haki saï. Speak true. When was the last time you saw him, and had you already given him those pills ?

– I saw him for the last time yesterday morning , at around nine o'clock. He told me to quickly pack my bags and leave. When I came back down, he was gone, and I never saw him again. That's the mystery. Since he was only sick during the night, what did he do all day long ? Why didn't he come back for me ? Do you know ?

I am the one who questions, but without getting an answer.

– Eight days earlier, I had given him laxative pills, the same pills that all the women of the harem, from the slaves to the first wife of the sub-governor, had successfully taken. You have the bottle with the power in it. There is even the address of the pharmacy in Suez. These are remedies; examine them.

And the day goes on like that, in front of this police chief, hysterical, shouting without respite : "Haki saï".

Hypnotic maneuver, which, it seems, has its effect on the Arabs, but to which I remain insensitive.

Jaber Effendi comes to question me as well. The deputy director of the police is methodical.

He writes his questions on a large sheet of paper. Dr. Ibrahim works as best he can. Also, I demand to write, in front of the Arabic interrogatory, my answers in French. I am sure to avoid any discussion and any translation error. I end my statements by asking for the twentieth time a lawyer and a good interpreter.

I don't want to offend Dr. Ibrahim, but I tell him that my situation is too serious for me to spare anyone. I prove to him that he doesn't understand the value of words and that bothers me.

Each moment brings me a little more discouragement. The

delegate from France is not coming. I wait in increasing nervousness. The slightest click of heels and rifles makes me shudder, but alas ! it's always the Arab people who parade by, and the day goes by without any news from outside. What will be done with me tonight ?

The hypnotic torture session and the interrogation ended at about eight o'clock in the evening, on the good word of Dr. Ibrahim :

– It is fortunate for you that Soleiman is not dead, which would have singularly aggravated your case...

– Of course. He will be able to certify that I did not give him any red powder. So I'm going to get my freedom back ?   And what reparations will I demand ?

– Nothing. If you are free, you will be happy enough not to ask for more.

I have an unspeakable fear of the night falling in the midst of my fearsome guardians. I implore Saïd bey to let me return to sleep in Ali Allmari's harem.

He answers me with a smile : "But yes, naturally," while I hear Jaber Effendi, indignant, protesting: "I will never let her out of here," and he makes a phonecall to the Emir of Djeddah to find out what he should do with the "Zeinab woman".

The answers are not very reassuring.

I hear : "Down there ? but there are about twenty priso-ners".

Then, turning to the police :

– Is it clean down there ?

Negative gestures of the "chaouichs".

– Remove the men, set up the room, orders Jaber Effendi, and take her there.

They are leaving. A moment goes by and, as soon as they come back up, a brief command :

– Guard, take the prisoner away.

For the first time, I implore, I ask to spend the night in the office of the police director, on a chair, on the floor, anywhere. But I dread the black dungeon. They formally refuse. In spite of my despair and fear, I no longer insist, because I feel them all unshakeable.

Weapons, sticks and heels rattling, I'm the one who's locked up.

Without resisting, I let myself be led, powerless to change my new destiny. The idea of an escape attempt touches me for a moment, but I quickly give up this hope, crossing a first small hall where there are a few armed policemen and a whole assortment of weapons. On the floor, sitting, lying down, standing, are prisoners on whom I stumble. They have just been evacuated from the room that has been reserved for me. Here it is. It is a kind of wet tomb, built half on stilts.

Never should I have imagined such an out-of-the-way place, the ceiling is covered with a kind of black muslin of cobwebs, which hang in stalactites over a thickness of at least one meter. This oozes moisture into viscous droplets that hang from the ceiling like liquid warts. As for the floor, humid, sticky, it is made of old planks, pierced in places with large holes where the whole foot can pass through. At every step, we slide on all kinds of rubbish left by my predecessors. A fetid, asphyxiating smell turns my heart, especially since I have been without food for 24 hours... The guards put a small lamp in a corner and leave me to this stench after having closed the two leaves of the shaky door, tied with a cord.

Terrified and helpless, I stand in front of the door, unable to sit or lie down in this garbage.

And the night begins. A sound of wings, followed by a shock against my body, abruptly pulls me out of my torpor, then another, and so on at the rate of one per minute, on my head, my chest, my legs. I was targeted by huge brown cockroaches, of the flying species that we have in the East. Every time I flinched, I grabbed the lamp, hoping to protect myself by moving. I walk carefully through this sludge of human residues; my first step, at the edge of a hole, makes a cloud of these horrible beasts, as if moved by a mechanical spring. Paralyzed by terror, I remain in place, projecting light around my cell. The show finishes me off, an army of cockroaches takes possession of the prison, the walls look alive under this brown swarm. In the corners, eyes shine, rats, hallucinating insects gush out between the wall and the poorly joined planks. Soon I crush on my veil and my dress the thousands of bugs that run and hide among the folds... Spiders, as big as crabs, cling with their claws on my flesh...

A bland, unhealthy wind blows violently towards the floor. An unspeakable terror hugs me. I am afraid. There are degrees in fear as in all things. But, at this hour, it is in me at its highest degree. It seizes me with its procession of shivers, monstrous horrors, paralysis, absurd sensations and faltering will. A cold sweat floods me. I want to scream, my voice stops in my throat, I have no more saliva, no more blood, my body stiffens. I feel myself going crazy, while the cockroaches are waging a merciless war on me, on the ground and in the air. Not content with hitting me in the face, they climb up my legs, and huge fleas eat me under my clothes.

This is how the night is spent. Standing, sometimes on one leg, sometimes on the other, I touch the borders of anguish and horror. I close my eyes so that I can no longer see anything. The soldiers sing gloomy and monotonous tunes that keep me in agony. Twice my door yielded, under the pressure of the prisoners whose place I took. A shaggy head falls to the floor with a crash; soon after, it is the fuzzy head of a large black man. The cord had yielded, but a guard reattached it. After being seized by the appearance of these wild and unexpected skulls, this moment of interruption in my solitude is a joy.

Several times the "chaouichs" open to contemplate me in silence and make sure that I am not evaporated. Each time it's a new shock because I expect the worst.

The guard changes. Noises take on a threatening value in this silence; it seems that great executions are being prepared. And the hours go by, long, endless. I don't even hear the "muezzin". The day also seems never to dawn again. At last a dawn glow appears in the window. Is it a miracle ? No, the day rises slowly, enters my prison, while the carpet of cockroaches disappears among a thousand holes with the night.

I feel immediately comforted by the clarity. I am also burning with fever. I take a few steps, my swollen feet hurt and my head is spinning. In a last effort, I climb up a wall to raise my face to the height of the bars of my window and I call the sentry, I beg this soldier to let me go up to the interrogation room where I will get some fresh air. Here I absorb poison. The answer is what it was supposed to be :

"Sabour ! Patience !" Always the same old refrain, a man would be dying that, for fear of making a decision, one would finish him off with this word :

"Sabour ! Patience !"

Still standing at my window, raising me on the tiptoes to flee the smell of my dungeon, I see the Egyptian and Italian consulates barely two hundred meters away.

Men breathe the morning breeze on their balconies.

I need to get their attention at all costs. Believing I have been spotted, I join my hands in a gesture of supplication. Pain lost, they disappear and I remain alone, disappointed behind my bars. They have probably not even been able to see me, because I don't dare to move my arms forward because of the guard.

My body is covered with stings, as numerous as the pores of my skin. I scratch myself to the blood to satisfy the itching that assails me. At nine o'clock, a guard comes to pick me up to take me upstairs where the interrogation continues.

I breathe a sigh of relief.

Jaber Effendi and Dr. Ibrahim cannot give me any news about Soleiman.

They did not go to the hospital.

The questionnaire is so monotonous, it's such a repetition of identical formulas that I refuse to repeat the same thing over and over again, and I write as an answer to several similar questions : "I have answered".

I ask with great insistence to be confronted with Soleiman. They oppose a force, of desperate inertia, and postpone this interview that I always believe is possible. I beg to be allowed to see the consul or someone who has close contact with the king. I will entrust to them, I say, a secret and the whole affair will be cleared up, and then I will be free. My interlocutors are very upset that I don't want to tell them this. How, by the way, can I explain my situation to them ? The white marriage that I had contracted is unknown to them, the Koran forbids it. But I hope that more civilized people could understand it. I may be wrong...

Saïd bey arrives. He brings reassuring news about the state of Soleiman. I dread and long to see him, thinking that my deliverance will follow automatically. At lunchtime my vigilantes finally leave, without having decided anything, and I foud out through the "chaouich" that all the prisoners are fed by their families. Alas ! mine doesn't know where I am (fortunately) and it's a bit far away...

Besides, I am not hungry. My throat is tight and my stomach is closed. This drama, which I keep hoping will end, terrifies me in spite of everything. Prisoners in general do not rot in prison. They are quickly judged; after two or three days at the most, and it's an incessant coming and going.

In criminal matters, the old Koranic law is applied. Murder results in death; the head is cut off for an ordinary crime; for adultery, a more serious crime, death with torment; theft results in the loss of one or two limbs, right hand or left foot, or vice versa, depending on the seriousness of the case.

During the interrogation, at the end of the afternoon, the faces, impassive as they were, become threatening.

And suddenly, Jaber Effendi exclaims :

– All your words and writings are lies, it was you who killed Soleiman to marry young Maigret.

– This is madness. I barely know him. The French are not like you, it takes them a long time, months of conversation with someone to love them, and also time before marrying

them.

Jaber Effendi moves the head negatively.

But how can we make people, who marry twelve year old girls they have never seen, understand our morals ? As much as I explain that it is not enough to have met four or five times to marry someone, my listeners doubt all my words.

I add that Maigret is so young that he could be my son.

Nothing changes their opinion.

– There are mothers who do things with their sons, insists with dignity and lowering his eyes, Jaber Effendi.

THE HOUSE OF THE DEAD

HOW TO DISCUSS WITH THESE MUSLIMS fanatics, with invincible prejudices ?

Jaber Effendi affirms again, sure of the scope of his accusation :

– A man, in the great pains of death, does not lie, and Soleiman has named you.

– Since he is better, it was not the great pains of death, and before me he will never say that.

– He's dead, answer in chorus Doctor Ibrahim and Jaber Effendi.

– Is this true ? Is it true ?

– Yes...

– But when ? And why did you lie to me ? Saïd bey said he was getting better.

– He died the night you were arrested.

– Give me the details !

– He swallowed the poison around ten o'clock and by midnight he was dead.

I suddenly consider the new aspect of my situation and I try one last question :

– Did he say : "I am dying because of Zeînab or Zeînab killed me ?"

– Why ?

– The difference is total : if he said he was dying because of me, it's true, because I was the one who dragged him on this journey, but I know that he didn't say that I gave him the poison.

My plea relaxes these serious figures and Jaber Effendi, laughing, retaliates :

– You're a lawyer, you don't need one to defend yourself, you're clever.

– I want one, I am not familiar with your laws, and my loneliness depresses me more than anything else.

My coldness, however, in the face of the tragic news, surprises those who are accustomed to the pathetic demonstrations of these women from the East. The perceptive Jaber Effendi whispers :

– They say he wasn't your husband !

– No, I confessed. That's the secret I wanted to tell to the king or the minister of France. It was a marriage without carnal fulfillment. In France, we call it a "white marriage". I had taken Soleiman only to travel. His brothers and my servants from Palmyra know it and will be able to testify it. This explains my innocence. Why would I have killed him ? I was free in the end. It was I who was in command and I would not have suppressed him at the moment of accomplishing this journey that I ardently desired and for which I made so many sacrifices.

"I appeal to the intelligence of the judges. It is not only the absence of evidence : no one can find a plausible motive for this act of which I am accused."

With phlegm, Dr. Ibrahim resumes :

– So be it ! But you know the law of the Koran; when a dying man names his murderer, there is no need for a judgment or a witness to condemn him to death.

I protest :

– Soleiman did not name me, I said it when I thought he was alive, I repeat it now that he is dead.

– A man was found in your room.

– Yes ! but, in the eyes of the French, it is quite natural for a woman to spend the evening with a friend.

– You are no longer French, you are Nedjian and muslim.

– Muslim, yes ! Nedjian, no, I don't yet know your country and almost not your language.

– Adultery is in any case punishable by death among muslims. And adultery is when a woman is with a man other than her husband.

– The man is condemned to death, and the woman ?

– Women too...

I understood, it's death for me. I guess in these three words my certain condemnation.

– How will they kill me ?

– It is delicate. Women hardly ever leave the harems, two hundred years have passed since the last ones were executed. We still don't know how you will be killed. Usually men get their necks cut off, but it is a disgrace for an Arab to cut off a woman's neck. We'll probably do the simulacrum, after we get you on your knees in the public square.

"Then the man breaks his sword on his knee".

"For the adulterous woman like you, it is customary to be stoned to death after walking around the city in chains. All the inhabitants throw stones at her until she dies."

Enough ! I can't take it anymore. My tempes are beating, my ears are buzzing, stoned, stoned ...

I don't care about death, the neck slashed, shot, but stoned to death, how many hours of suffering... I dread that.

No more answer, two hard, closed, impassive beings look at me. They have nothing more to add. My mind refuses at this moment to conceive of the coming death : DEATH !

I go down like an automaton, I find myself in the darkness of my dungeon, in the middle of worms and filth. Exhausted, I crouch in this filth. What does it matter to me now ? It's all over, I don't even need to eat, and above all I don't want to ask for anything. Rats, fleas, ants, bedbugs, spiders, cockroaches are attacking me again. It's a kind of nightmare with no way out, vague, barely interrupted by a few moments of lucidity where I regret not having my neck sliced instead of the slow and atrocious agony of this lapidation.

Part of the night is spent in this painful annihilation, but, in the long run, the nervous shocks produced by the cockroaches hitting me make me react. I want to hope. I need to see my family again. Escape, almost impossible, is yet my only chance of salvation.

I feel all the iron bars, they are strong, the door is easy to open, but behind them are the condemned and the sentries, guards, soldiers and policemen. A hole in the wall ? With what ? And then, they are more than 60 centimeters thick.

What remains is the ground, this ground already dug everywhere, with, underneath, what ? the void ? or the sea I can hear ?

I pull the iron of an old lock that doesn't work out of the door and use it as a lever to lift a plank, two planks. It takes me a long time to get this poor result. My distress is at its height when I realize that four big walls are closing the underside of my prison. The waves die against these gnawed but iron-clad walls. Nothing, nothing, I cannot hope for anything and I cannot resign myself.

In the morning, I find the strength to climb up to the grid of the high window to breathe deeply. Arabs pass by. Weak, haggard, I look at these men dressed in dresses and with long falling curls. They impress me : are they real ? Where am I ? What is this race ? I am going crazy, yes, really crazy. And now I am no longer afraid of either day or night, but I am afraid of losing my mind, my poor head bursting. It must be noon, the sun is very high...

LIFE IN PRISON

I CALL A GUARDIAN TO REQUEST A doctor. I feel like I'm losing my mind. I'm also so swollen from the bites of all the bugs that I can't stand upright. My arms and legs are covered at the joints with a crust of clotted blood.

– Sabour ! Patience !

Finally, after three days of deadly waiting, a new hope was born in me. I am told that someone will come to see me in the evening.

I am counting the hours, and I am so tired and weak that I don't know if I am still thinking. Around five o'clock, I'm sent upstairs. Obviously they are ashamed to bring someone into my disgusting hovel.

Upstairs, a terrible disappointment, I find myself in the presence of a nurse from the "Frigi", a French ship that is currently in harbour, who has been called in. She is the only French woman in Djeddah. She hadn't even been down there and the story of my adventure hardly made her want to visit the port.

This person who was terrorized by the mission she was in charge of, and probably by the horrors she had been told about me, seemed stupid and heartless to me.

To everything I asked, and God only knows if I had exciting questions to ask, she would answer :

– I came to see how you are doing.

I put my hands on hers.

– You have a fever, she says. Do you need anything ?

– But everything ! I have nothing to drink, nothing to eat, nothing to wash, no bed. I would like some mineral water, I wrote to the king, to the consul to get some. I am going to die of thirst and nobody answers me.

She then assures me that she will pass on my requests, then leaves.

I had put so much secret hope in this visit that I feel overwhelmed.

And my daydreaming resumes, hallucinating, frantic, disheartened.

I'd rather be executed right away than to live in this tortured state, locked up, deprived of everything and with no news of anyone. I think of my mother, today is the anniversary of her death, one more sadness fills my soul. Soon I will join her.

And the night begins with its anguish, its terror, its noises, the vermin waking up.

At times the confidence comes back to me, because I can't stay sad for long, but at other times I really feel like dying.

From the first day of my arrest, I had tried to contact the Minister by a means that I cannot mention here, as all the people involved in this story are still alive. Today I am certain that the Consul received my call; I begged him as always to come and see me, adding that I was covered in bruises.

In the afternoon, my door opened and gives way to Jaber Effendi and the nurse.

She questions according to the protocol they probably imposed on her :

– The Minister of France sent me to check up on you.

– I am not well.

– Have you been beaten ?

– No.

– So what are you complaining about ? You're very "lucky".

Certainly, I understand that one cannot extend one's sympathy to infinity and that most humans only have a limited amount of feelings to offer to other beings.

All the same, this icy indifference drives me crazy. Does this person really believe that I killed Soleiman and deems me criminal or is it a natural dryness of heart on her part ?

I find in front of me, at a tragic hour of my destiny, the same widespread mediocrity and the same inability to see anything but platitude and conformism. And I suffer from it as I have always suffered from it, but with what acuity !

This hardness and misunderstanding exasperated me and I shout :

– I would like mineral water, a bowl, soap, a bed, food.

Okay, we'll send you everything you need.

She said the same thing to me the day before and I'm still waiting. I show her again, my swollen and prick-covered legs.

– It's the fleas, she says coldly.

– Why doesn't the minister come to see me ? Does he think I'm guilty ? Will he see me if I escape ?

– I don't know anything, and, she adds as she heads for the door, it's my last visit, the boat leaves tomorrow.

Suddenly, facing her, I hand her a letter for the consul, imploring him to have me executed quickly. She retreats. Her terror, her stupidity make her decline my request, she turns to Jaber Effendi, looking for his authorization. But he, with his bright eyes, has already spotted the message and grasps it.

I return to my cell without looking at this disgusting person, paralyzed by fear, who in such a situation was unable to say a comforting word to me, was unable to make a gesture to help me.

Now I think of the Hindu of the journey from Suez to Djeddah, who knew how to find for all the distant miseries of the world, the word that heals, the formula that sympathizes, the very gesture, the modest gesture that nevertheless relieves.

But these enslaved souls that the West is manufacturing, deprived of all individuality, of all generosity, make life more atrocious for the imprisoned woman that I am.

This obnoxious visit took away my last courage. Now all I have left to do is write. To write to all those who at this moment have my fate, my life.

The truth is, I'm waiting to die. Writing makes me forget the monstrous images that are beginning to haunt me. And it is a letter to the consul to ask to bring my son, if there is time before my execution, another to Ibn Saud, another to Fouad Hamza, his Minister of Foreign Affairs. Since I must die, I beg them to hurry, to spare me these awful days and nights of vigil haunted by hideous nightmares.

Alas ! the word fast and the idea of speed are unknown to the Arabs. My letters leave, but silence follows them.

And a new night returns, the fifth in this prison, again the vermin devour my wounds. The day rises again and the consul does not come.

On Wednesday, April 26, I feel excruciatingly weak. I haven't eaten anything in five days. My chaouichs pity me. This pity has not penetrated the ship's infirmary. But they are going to buy me some bread, some lében (curdled milk), some tea, always so good in the East.

In spite of my weakening, I would like to support myself in order to avoid the madness that is bothering me and that I fear more than anything else. In the following night, there are next to me the sounds of chains and weapons. The great crimi- nels are taken to Mecca by truck. The unfortunate do not have long to suffer any more. My fear is to be sent there as well.

At first, the promiscuity with the bandits in this prison horrified me, but I got used to their melancholy songs. Now that they're going to "taste death", I miss them. The idea of being executed and even stoned is already atrocious. However, waiting for the unknown day of this torture is abominable. It is a moral torture in which one always feels on the verge of insanity.

And I cry.

I mourn those whom I love, whom I will never see again and who will never know the final word of this oriental tragedy. People will say : "murder and adultery" and many will believe it.

I am writing a farewell letter to my son. I explain the facts to him. The true facts that are certainly drowned at this very hour in Djeddah in a heap of lies and absurd inventions. I must say here, marginally, that the High Commission in Beirut received this letter in its time, but they never gave it to my son who resided in that city.

I finally found a way to leave my dungeon several times a day. It's nothing, but it's a kind of temporary escape...

Because, for natural needs, I am granted the right reserved to the chief of police.

Of course, I always go there under escort, between two sentries, bayonet to the gun, and it is a simple pit on the Red Sea. It may be difficult, however, to get people to grasp what comfort it gives me. And yet...

Through the skylight of this small isolated corner, I can see the sea, the consulate, the French flag.

The sight of this flag moves me deeply to tears.

I would like answers to my letters, because the most painful thing is not knowing anything.

I am writing to the Emir of Djeddah.

But neither he, nor Fouad Hamza, nor Ibn Saud give me any sign of life. It is true that I write to them in French. And then, do they receive these letters ?

Two days after my arrest, Saïd bey was dismissed. The new director of the police force often passes in front of my windows; he has never spoken to me. I try to pity Jaber Effendi. I ask him to give me Soleiman's suitcase, his large abayes, his cape coat that I could use as a pillow. But I am tacitly refused all this.

On April 29, the consulate sent me chops and mineral water. In my situation, the slightest bit of sweetness is a great luxury.

Hope returns to me. Sometimes, I renounce everything, I shovel the death that will allow me the supreme journey and to have the great word of the beyond, this definitive departure. Sometimes I would like to live and come out innocent of this trap, to return to embrace those I love.

On April 30, Jaber Effendi brings me the Life of Mohammed, seized from my suitcase and which I have been claiming since my incarceration.

I read amazing things. Examples of Arab warriors' that encourage me to die like them.

Here is an absolutely heroic one :

"At the battle of Ohod, the third year of the hegira, the Quoraichite standard bearer is killed, several men succeeded him and die in their turn. A

young Abyssinian slave seizes the flag, immediately Saad ben Ali Vaqqac cuts off his right hand, he grabs his left hand, this one in turn is cut off, he then squeezes the flagpole of his stumps, but he is literally chopped into pieces with a sword. Throwing himself upon the standard to cover it with his body, he dies crying, "Have I done all my duty ?"

I feel very down, tired of waiting.

At the beginning I watched the water carriers, the divers and the Blacks going into the sea with their henna-dyed donkeys. The small Javanese boys with narrow hips, tightly wrapped in plaid or brightly striped loincloths, entertained me a lot. They went from the port to the Dutch legation and the prison is in their way. But now I meditate on the awful forebodings of my real husband, Mrs. Amoun and the Italians on board of the Dandolo.

And my fear feeds on these dire predictions.

In the next room, new prisoners have been brought in. During the night, pressed on top of each other, they push my door open. They then slump down on the floor of my cell with a macabre noise. I tremble with fear. On the morning of May 1st, I find the bread I had put on the window all covered with ants. My guards, who showed me pity, advised me to surround my food supply with a small thread of oil. I do this. In my situation, you do whatever you are advised to do. But the ants of the Hedjaz are terrible beasts, the next day my food is still covered by them.

I have a headache and I'm itchy. They still bring me cookies and mineral water from the consulate. I drink tea, because the "kawagis" can, 4 or 5 times a day, sell this tea to the prisoners. I also eat olives.

One does not figure oneself, in the course of life, as it takes little to live.

In order not to go crazy, I give myself tasks to accomplish. I kill bedbugs, that could take up half a century. I also catch big spiders with fearsome beaks and I try to fill the holes in my floor with paper. But there comes a fetid wind from below, so strong that the paper is removed and gets caught in the cobwebs of the ceiling.

However my ailments take a bad turn. My skin goes away in pieces like that of lepers. They bring me Dr. Akram. He is a compassionate, sympathetic, very good man. He speaks good French and advises me to ask the Emir of Djeddah for my transfer to the hospital.

He then sends me talcum powder in a newspaper cone and petroleum jelly in a small cardboard jar. This attention touches me and gives me a very great softening. Until then I used to throw a little water on my swollen flesh to get a momentary respite, but then I felt worse pain and burning.

The consulate always sends me food, chops, roast mutton. But, despite my desire, I can hardly eat. Everything in me is constricted and refuses to function, especially my throat and my mouth.

In the afternoon I also receive fabric, thread, needles that I had asked for to keep me busy. I hem handkerchiefs.

May 3 - The miracle happens. Jaber Effendi presents me with a typewritten paper that says : "Tomorrow, at 4 p.m., the French delegate will come to see you".

My happiness is indescribable... after 13 days of waiting, I didn't hope anymore...

I expect everything from this visit. The total absence of information where I was, was the most painful thing that ever happened to me. My impotence was also a torture, I was burned with the desire to act and I could not do anything, letters, words, everything remained unanswered. For the Hijazis probably don't understand my letters. I counted the hours, the minutes, I watched through my bars, when Mr. Maigret finally arrived, escorted by members of the consulate

I am very moved, I can hardly say hello to him.

Mr. M. looks at me, not washed, not combed, gray skin, my arms peeling off in patches, and he says, "I expected to find you in a sad state, but I never thought it would be this bad".

His energetic and straightforward personality immediately gave me great confidence, I suddenly felt uplifted. He taught me that through my marriage I am subject to the laws of Hijaz and that he, at this moment, can do nothing for me. But he assures me that everything will go smoothly, that I will not be transported to Mecca, which has become an obsession for me.

There is no question of immediate execution, Mr. M. still certifies to me that an investigation is in progress, it is necessary to wait for the result.

– How long will the investigation take ?

– It depends, he says, some last a month, while others take six.

– I prefer death to six months in this dungeon. Couldn't you get me temporary release ?

– This is impossible, this case is not provided for by the laws of Hijaz.

Jaber Effendi is present at this interview, as he was at all those I had afterwards. So, approaching the consul, I whispered in his ear : "I really want to escape. If I arrive at your place, could you hide me ?"

– But you can't run away.

– I prefer all risks to this waiting, then I think I could fall into the sea, through the skylight of the W.C.; if I don't break anything, I will pass through a hole seen in the wall along the shore, I will arrive at the consulate, but would you keep me if I succeeded ?

– Don't try this madness, the road to the consulate is dominated by the police station, you would be shot. Even supposing that you were successful, which I don't think you would be, I would be obliged to hand you over to the authorities who, obviously, would demand you. You are Nedjienne and I cannot act for you officially. However, I will try to come and see you regularly.

– Oh yes, that's what I like the most, sir.

The consul, not being able to give me all the moral satisfactions, at least wants me to have all the material consolations.

Indeed, from the next day, the effect of his visit is felt.

They carry me a bed, a box of creoline, I spend the morning cleaning, I sprinkle everything copiously with this disinfectant, I sweep with palm leaves lent by a chaouich. I kill an army of bedbugs and ants, I see a night of uninterrupted sleep.

Mr. M... had also sent me a few books, but they had not been given to me. When I entered my room, he was holding two in his hand and they didn't dare to take them away from him. Jaber Effendi leafed through them with an inquisitive air and then left them with me. Lying on my little bed, I read with delight... I see, once again, that all good things are relative. A few days later, Mr. M... even sent me a rattan armchair. My comfort increased and above all I no longer felt abandoned. His authoritarian frankness, almost brutal in some ways, gave me hope. His mixture of gentleness and energy, his assurance that the happy outcome of this drama would soon come, did me the greatest good.

It's rare to meet a public servant of character, and I was sure that he would do everything he could to save me.

At the end of the day, a servant brings me my first full meal from the consulate. Eggs, fish and meat. All this on a large platter, on plates, which dazzles me as much as my captive neighbors. Jaber

Effendi presents the dishes before serving them to me; he lifts the plates; looks at them underneath, also under the tray and, when he is sure that no cabalistic signs adorn my dishes, a guard hands me my food.

I have lost my appetite and I give away half of my food to other captives with whom I sympathize. I finally fall asleep in bed !... barely worried about the future, all to the joy of the improvements that this day has brought me. And I thought, the first time I had to sleep in cotton sheets, that I would not be able to sleep, I don't realize tonight that these sheets are as new as waxed cardboard.

But I was awakened at about two or three o'clock in the morning by the preparations of an army of policemen on their way to meet the king, whose arrival is scheduled for this morning. At dawn, cannon shots were fired to welcome His Majesty, while I saw the green Nedjian flag against my bars. All the legations have also raised their large flags. These patches of color brighten my sight and I contemplate them at length.

The day is dull, I hem handkerchiefs and only think about the visit of the consul, announced for the next day. All the time of my captivity, it will be my only ray of sunshine. A handsome black servant brings me my food every day. My attempts to keep anything, for the evening or for the next day, are fruitless. The beasts seem to have disappeared, but the slightest victuals attract myriads of them. My janitor Naser has the good initiative of stretching a rope from one end of my room to the other, attached to the wall with nails. On the rope we hang two small wicker baskets where I put my bread, sugar, milk, etc. I am saved, I cover each basket with a paper to avoid the fall of flying insects and I am in a relative state of cleanliness.

I want to adjust my rope, like all my other little things so far, and even my water to wash myself. But I am generously told that the Government offers me this; later the water was given to me... The remedies too, Dr. Akram says that the Ministry of Hygiene gives me this gift....

May 10 - Night of insomnia, nightmare, I'm afraid the consul won't come. From three o'clock on, I keep a lookout. He finally arrives around 4:30, when I almost despair. He still has the words that make me feel good. He cheers me up, he really thinks it won't be long now. He still carries me fabric, a few pounds, milk cans. I ask him if he has informed Beirut of my arrest, but his answers are terse : I did what I needed to do where I needed to do it, with whom I needed to do it.

I insist, he is stubborn in a mystery and a discre- tion that makes me tense.

All these details interest me; they would please me, sir. I wish to be informed. But, supposedly in my interest, Mr. M... doesn't want to tell me anything, it is very painful.

May 11 - I have a tub (a large Arabic dish), water, and I take pleasure in washing myself every morning. I often ask to go to the toilet on the sea. I stay there as long as possible to breathe and enjoy the freedom. An ocean liner appears on the horizon, will I get any news from it ?

EXPECTATIONS

I'M STARTING TO HOPE, BUT THE HUMAN being is difficult to satisfy. Now this hope is aimed at what yesterday I thought was just unattainable : it is freedom I need.

Now the consulate sends me exquisite things, cakes, small onions or breaded chops. Hamdi bey even makes me take part in the sending of beets from Suez, what a privilege to have vegetables in the burning Arabia !

Tonight, surprise : at seven o'clock, I am already exhausted and I am about to forget in my sleep my situation and its dangers, when the deputy director of the police enters with rage. He rushes to my bed as if he wants to devour me. I shiver. So that he thus loses all control of itself, it must be serious. This is surely the fatal moment. Not at all. He wants Soleiman's "abaye".

I don't understand. I have never had any of my passport husband's clothes here. I explain that Soleiman's effects must be in his suitcase and I finally fall asleep.

A fixed idea tortures me now, to get out of my dungeon. Certainly, I know the relief that has come to attenuate the rigor of the beginning. If, moreover, it had continued, I would have been condemned, for I felt the wing of the madwoman brush past me several times. But, at this hour, this life seems to me like a decline, and the horror that I have of it, like a fixed idea, fills my soul day and night.

I struggle by making hems on handkerchiefs. But it's a remedy that alleviates the pain without making me forget it. I have hemmed 63 extremely fine handkerchiefs in my prison.

Each visit to the toilet awakens my hopes, my need to escape. However, where to go ? No consulate will keep me, everywhere I will be found. One hour after my escape, I will be reported, wherever I am, and picked up again, then...

A terrible discouragement seizes me, no reasoning helps me, any beneficial reaction is condemned in advance ...

Visit of Mr. M... who makes me understand that I will soon be questioned. I await this moment with feverish impatience. I spend my day reading the frivolous life of an actress of the Comédie Française during the war. The atmosphere of the book is so different from what I know today that I feel a little like I'm walking into a fairy tale. I still read the White Squadron, by Peyré, a fellow countryman ! And I wait for the convocation of the cadi, but nothing happens. How many more days will it take ?

I write to the Emir, asking him to hasten the investigation and asking him to let me know if Soleiman really accused me before he died, I can't believe it.

For nights and days I have been searching for the riddle of the last day. Where has he been ? What has he done ? Why didn't he wait for me after he told me to pack my bags quickly and leave ?

I'm not accusing anyone, but since he was bragging about having made a colossal wedding, wouldn't he have been killed in the hope of stealing it ?

I call Jaber Effendi to send me to the cadi.

He is beginning to be jaded to my pleas and doesn't even come down anymore.

At the end of the day the consul visits me, accompanied by his secretary and Hamdi bey. They exhort me to be patient and explain to me that the longest time has passed. The consul tells me that my French husband, the real one, is in Beirut, with our friends Seyrig. That was all. Not another word. I am worried about my husband's anguish, about my sons... what do they know ? My sorrow is increased by all the ignorance that torments me. I have never received a letter. I've never been given a newspaper, we've asked several times for permission to receive periodicals, it's strictly forbidden.

Dr. Akram paid me a visit. I complain about my leg, my teeth, I look for any excuse to fight against this dull loneliness that wears me out and destroys me piece by piece. Akram assures me that the only thing left is the result of an analysis of Soleiman's stomach, gastric juice and viscera, which is done in Egypt. It still happens quite often that boats arrive in Djeddah, but they are Hindu, Russian, etc. So I am only looking for those from Suez. They may be liberating.

May 15 - The entire police building is paved for the arrival of Seoudi, the king's eldest son.

An other visit from the consulate, which does not bring me any news. I ask Hamdi bey the permission to breathe some air on the balcony at nightfall. The authorization is granted, but in the evening, when I want to use my new rights, Jaber Effendi opposes it on the pretext that he must consult the Moudir Cherta. For three days, I ask every evening, until the formal refusal. I would have liked to reduce the length of the nights, they are eternal, it's dark at 7 o'clock, and escape a little from the fetid and unhealthy smells that will suffocate me throughout my captivity.

My "chaouich" explains to me that on the balcony I could be seen, but it is not appropriate to expose a woman in an open space when the whole building contains only men. Their prejudices live on.

May 20 - I am very down again, at the end of my resistance, I ask again for Dr. Akram who, unwillingly his terrible aspect is sympathetic to me. He always has encouraging words. I announce a new pain in any part of my body. In reality, I have seen boats. I think they come from Suez. I always hope for good news and I question my rare visits as much as possible. It's terribly hot, everyone complains, one guard is dizzy. He falls down on the prisoners as I go back in. Miraculously, his bayonet slips on the bare chest of one of them, who is also lying on the ground. I love this temperature; when everyone asks me how I can stand it, it's the least of my worries.

The consulate sends me the combs I asked for to hold my hair, because it is getting long and falling on my shoulders; I don't have a mirror and my toiletries are very precarious.

Dr. Akram came to examine me with a pharmacist who was at the American University of Beirut. He knows Dr. Escher, a friend of mine from Syria. Here we are in a country of knowledge. They talk to me about 15 more days of waiting. Alas ! I have no more patience. The pharmacist sends me a potion to calm my nerves. I do not drink it. The legation has, at my request, given me an English dictionary to work with this language, but my poor head is in such a state that I cannot fix my mind.

Otherwise, the prison would obviously be the ideal place for study.

One of Ali Allmari's little slaves comes to see me with Sett Kebir's son. I embrace them, so happy to see friendly figures. The whole harem, it seems, thinks of me. Sett Kebir sends me honey from Medina. She is touching and I like her. The little slave Ahmed makes me tense, because his inferior being brain hardly inspires him. Wanting to be kind, he breaks our silences with the Arabic leit-motive that we place several times in each conversation : "Enta mabsout ?"

"Are you happy ?"

At the third time, I end up bursting :

– Shut up, Ahmed, no ! I am not happy, alone, locked up, unhappy.

But he doesn't understand and looks at me with his huge eyes always amazed.

– Isn't that the classic, polite question that we ask everyone ?

– Not to me, in my situation, Ahmed.

May 23 - I find at the bottom of a shoe a box of cutex nailpolish forgotten by the analysis. I rub my nails for hours. At night, I break my lamp glass. One goes quickly, in spite of the late hour, to get me another one ? I had to pray forcefully to my guardian, because I would be too afraid to spend the night in darkness. Ali Abdou, a guy from Djibouti, rushed. As soon as I was a little familiar with my guards, they were all perfect in their correctness, exactness, politeness.

The Wahhabi police force is impeccable, and these men, who are hard on their fellow men, have shown me these delicacies, these kindnesses that only come from the heart. Even the prisoners whom I often had to step over to cross the hall always kept the best behavior. Can you imagine what such promiscuity would have been like in Europe ?

Thursday, May 25 - Around 11:00 a.m., an unknown guard tells me to get dressed to appear before the cadi. I tremble, but I leap for joy. Whatever happens, I will be able to leave these places that I loathe. But alas, after the classic questionnaire of surname, first names, etc. place of residence, the cadi, without a word, raises the hand, and Dr. Akram, the interpreter, tells me it's over.

I would like to be questioned again to undermine their hesitations, I no longer thought of going back to prison, but to go straight back home in France.

I insist ardently.

In eight or ten days you will come back, said Akram, we must first get this answer from Egypt.

– Mercy, mercy, I would like to justify myself, get it over with.

– Sabour, patience.

In the evening, visit of two members of the consulate, the minister could not come. He is ill. He has a high fever. He is tired from the heat... Dark presentiments... My imagination is in delirium, he is going to be poisoned, he is going to die and all my hope is in him !

May 26 - They bring me a table. The government has been a long time before allowing, in a prison, this luxury object... a small white wooden table... I clean my whole cell with creoline, because spiders seem to have reproduced en masse these last days. My guards are swooning over my installation.

– You're like a schoolmaster, they exclaim. In fact, I am sadly sitting in front of my little table, but this posture is unknown in Hedjaz. Only teachers and some ministers sit on a chair in front of tables. Usually you are on the floor or crouching on benches, like sofas, which surround almost every room. Jaber Effendi himself, the most sincere of all, raves : "What a beautiful room !" I laugh in spite of my distress.

Every fortnight, a slender man, very tanned, bare legs and draped in white, sings in the streets to a strange rhythm. I get informed. He announces the arrivals and departures of the boats, he lists the names and ports where the ship will call. He replaces the poster, the advertisement, the information agency, he also gives the departure tickets.

Leaving... departure... what words ! I shudder.

Sunday, May 26 - I'm exhausted again, by this perpetual waiting.

I don't know. Mr. M... himself doesn't tell me much. What weakness ! What impotence ! In these moments of revolt, I understand the hatred of the prisoner for the man on the outside who does not understand that freedom is the only asset in the world, since all hopes and ambitions are allowed to the free man and everything is denied to the prisoner.

I have a crisis of atrocious despair. I burst into tears. But instead of hiding, I call my guards, tell them that I'd rather die, I call the deputy director of police. I bang my head against the walls, against the iron bars. I hope to soften Jaber Effendi with my tears and make him more human. But the effect is the opposite of what I expected. He blames me for my tears, asks me if I am not ashamed to cry like this.

– No, no, I'm not ashamed, I'm too unhappy.

– Well, if you continue, you'll get the worst punishment : you'll be locked up far away, in a dark room, without air, very hot, very dirty...

– Great God, what could be worse than mine ?

– You will be deprived of visits from the consul.

– I am at peace. He will come from far away to see me, he has his car and I trust him, he will not abandon me.

The struggle rekindled my courage. I prefer to let this hard-hearted being go.

– Go away, since you're so mean, I won't ask you for anything more.

Then, an inexplicable turnaround occurs. For the first time, Jaber Effendi seems to be moved.

– Are you a mother ?

– Yes.

– You have to live for your children.

– I will not live if you prolong my captivity too long.

– The cadi is sick, that is what delays your judgment; as soon as he is better, you will be called and your judgment will be his first job, the king has ordered it.

At last some information. Everything is indifferent to me from now on and I would like my fate, whatever it was, to be decided very quickly. To know, to know.

May 29 - Horrible fright in the night. I woke up with a start. A shotgun explodes in the convicts' hall : shouting, screaming, complaints, jostling. I shout. One of my faithful guards, to reassure me, comes in, he tells me that a gun has fallen to the ground, that the shot went off alone...

In all countries the police lie is the same.

On the evenings when I feel too nervous, when the anxiety is choking me, my guardian stands against my door outside and sings these monotones, gutturals Arabic tunes but which are my narcotics and which I can no longer do without. And it's a sweetness to feel this friendly heart singing behind my door to tell me : "I'm here, I'm protecting you, I'm guarding you".

THE JUDGMENT

THE CADI IS STILL SICK. YET, THIS EVENING, the consul did certify me that my ordeal will soon be over.

He has told me this many times before, but this time I want to believe him.

May 31 - Visit of Lotfi. I'm told that in reality the cadi has gone to Mecca to render a judgment.

June 5 - Jaber Effendi tells me that the cadi will not return for another ten days. My despair is reborn and growing.

June 8 - Mr. M... gives me good news. But I have suffered so many disappointments after my rancid hopes that I now doubt everything.

Ibn Saud's private secretary is said to have said that my case is over and that my release is imminent.

June 9 - Sabour. Waiting, always waiting, in terrible anguish and when everything in you revolts against this miserable immobility.

Jaber Effendi tells me through the gates that the cadi has entered. Hope is reborn in me.

Saturday, June 10 - The king arrived at 6 a.m., greeted by a salvo of artillery. I don't doubt for a moment that he gave the cadi the order to free me.

Mr. M... told me so much that I will be free.

Once again, I'm wrong. All administrative formalities, on the contrary, are stopped by the coming of the king. He summons all his functions and receives all his subjects.

By the bearer of my lunch, I ask the consul for an additional visit because I am so tired. But he too went to greet the king.

I am expecting everything from His Majesty's arrival; it now seems to delay my release, unless I am deluded and this coming brings me closer to death. I would like to fall asleep and wake up only when a decision is made, my strength of resignation is at its limit. Fear that they have been hidden from me a terrible fate in order to let me believe until the end in an impossible liberation.

I suddenly have an abominable crisis. All that remains of my recent rancid hopes is an atrocious bitterness. At first I accepted the worst, while waiting, after a hundred promises, for a freedom that perhaps will be denied me... The Minister, Mr. M., told me :

"Even if they take you to the firing squad, don't be afraid", What does he mean ?

Towards the end of the day, I receive an unexpected visit from the consul who, believing that I had seen the cadi, comes to inquire about this interview.

The interrogation cannot be delayed any longer.

Monday, June 12 - I wake up very early, very agitated. Yet I need to stay calm. At around 10 a.m., I am ordered to prepare to appear before the cadi, the great judgment will begin. I leave for the court between the king's guards, on foot and veiled.

Tragedy ! The interrogation is postponed to the next day, the interpreters are missing.

However, I am hopeful for the next day. But I am constantly oscillating between opposing feelings, and the only real satisfaction I feel is to imagine my pleasure when I am finally free, if I am free at all...

Tuesday, June 13 - At 9 o'clock, I get impatient and ask again to appear before the cadi. The interpreters have not arrived. The wait is impossible. At ten o'clock, I leave on foot, veiled, flanked by my two policemen, bayonet to the barrel. The fresh air, the light, the space, the walk that I almost forgot give me physical pleasure. I feel full of courage and authority, ready to fight ferociously against the accusation that weighs on me.

The court is about ten minutes from the prison. The path runs along the consulates of Italy, England and Holland. The mere sight of these European pavilions rekindles my desire to escape. In one leap, I could pass through one of these doors. As my impulses are always as strong as my reasoning, I find it very difficult to dominate my ardent desire to escape. But what's the point of risking everything the moment I reach the goal ?

We finally arrive at this Nedjian courtyard that I have been longing for two months. The gate is guarded militarily by armed sentries. The cadi, being, hierarchically the highest ranking judge, is on the top floor. We go up by a small narrow staircase with very high steps. On each landing, armed policemen watch over three or four courts, before which common crimes are judged. A few more steps, and I find myself in a long, narrow room, lit by a large moucha-rabieh in front of which a small, thin and pale man is crouching on a bench, caressing his foot with one hand, while with the other hand he is fanning him-self, it is the cadi. The heat is suffocating.

The apparatus of justice is reduced to its simplest expression : a clerk and two interpreters, sitting on the same bench as the cadi, wait, dreaming. In front of the cadi, a table and, at the back on the right, two superb, muscular black men, dressed in small panties and yellow wrestler's jerseys. They look like a lost circus act. They are probably the executors of the sentences involving beatings with sticks...

Behind me the room comes alive, is filled with men of all classes, all colors who come to watch this sensational trial for Djeddah.

As I enter, the cadi slowly turns his head and examines me with a disquieting look. I remain veiled, which helps me to support the penetration of his eyes and to conceal my anguish.

The cadi starts the interrogation with the following question :

– Why are you in prison ?

I leap in shock at such an unexpected question.

– "Enta megnoun". You are crazy ! I've been in prison for two months and you ask me why ! Don't you know it, you, who made the investigation, you who must judge me ? I was told that before he died Soleiman had accused me of poisoning him and that's the reason I was given to keep me locked up.

The audience was astonished to hear a woman call the holiest magistrate in Djeddah a madman. Obviously, in a violent outburst, the word escaped me. The cadi did not flinch at the insult, and calm was restored, while he confirmed : "But yes, that's just why you were arrested." I later found out that my answer alone could have been the basis of the whole judgment. Indeed, if I had simply answered :

– For killing Soleiman.

This sentence would have been considered as a confession and I would have been condemned to death without any other subtlety of form. Such a question is classic in any Arab case and the first question asked to any accused. Often, it seems, he gets confused. Recently, in Algeria, the case arose of a man accused of stealing an ox, the judge asked him:

– Why are you in prison ?

– Because I stole a beef.

186

There, he confessed. He is condemned.

Then there are the eternal questions about Soleiman, the marriage, its conditions, the complete program of my jour-ney, the poison and the last moments of the poor man.

The lawyer of the opposing party, appointed by the government, is trying to trick me and confuse the dates on which I gave these famous Kalmine pills. I ask for my red notebook, on which all my actions are recorded day by day, to be returned to me so that I can have absolute precision. But the cadi is formally opposed to this.

To Mr. M... who, for a long time, asked for a lawyer for me, it was answered that I was eloquent enough to defend myself and I plead my case myself.

The lawyer maintains so forcefully that it was my remedies that killed Soleiman, that the cadi gave him until the next morning to prove it in court.

Hostile movements in the public.

I am staggering with rage, and all the forced inactivity of my detention suddenly spills over into the defense that I am putting to the prosecution. In a terrifying silence, I de-monstrate that it was impossible for me to hide any poison on me during my stay in Djeddah, since the women of the harem would attend my toilet and constantly see me naked.

As for using my suitcase, there had been no question of it, since it had been taken from the speedboat taking me to the port of Djeddah, and it had been searched at customs without my presence. Moreover, would I have taken poison in a suitcase that could not be locked ?

As for the last accusatory hypothesis, that of having bought poison in Djeddah, it could not be taken into consideration since I was never outside alone. Besides, I don't speak Hijaz Arabic well enough to get a forbidden product. An investigation on this subject would quickly inform the justice system.

As the interpreter translates, I watch the crowd, they seem visibly surprised by the situation that my plea creates.

The cadi remains crouched, impassive, fanning himself, then removing his small cap (kofia) to air his skull.

Several times I am interrupted and told to simply answer "yes" or "no", but I want to clarify.

I go on to explain that I had no reason to kill Soleiman. One resource to get rid of him remained : on my way home to Syria, I would have obtained a divorce very easily.

The cadi resumes in an insinuating voice :

– In the kingdoms of Nedj and Hijaz, divorce exists only at the request of the man. You didn't know this, you found it out in Djeddah and wanted to free yourself from it.

– I could escape anyway without killing him. The consul had advised me against this trip and would have had me boarded if I had asked him to leave.

I was the one who stubbornly wanted to cross the Nedj, to stay in Oneiza, to cross the Hofouf desert. I waited only for the king's permission to leave. Why would I have killed Soleiman before knowing the royal decision ?

I end my plea with my last, and perhaps strongest, argument by invoking as a witness the entire harem. How could I have given poison to a man with whom I did not eat my meals, with whom I did not live and whom I only saw face to face in an empty room at Ali Allmari's house ?

It would have been impossible and absurd to claim to force him, in this place, to take any food whatsoever.

The lawyer of the opposing party stands up and affirms that he cannot believe anything I say, that it was the Kalmine that killed Soleiman.

The interpreter declares on my behalf that this is impossible.

And the lawyer goes on to say :

– I'll give you the proof tomorrow.

This man is obnoxious. He deliberately confuses the dates, but in this case they are fortunately of no importance. I call him "kaseb" and "battal" - mean and liar. My interpreters, one of whom knows Paris and speaks excellent French, recommend moderation. The French Consul had told me that I could have complete confidence in these interpreters, Ibrahim Radwan and Negib Saleh, who, it must be said, were perfect, and it was their gentleness and understanding that encoura-ged me the most during the trial.

The hearing is adjourned.

I return to my dungeon. A mental reaction occurs : I suddenly feel exhausted and my head hurts to cry. And then, I had so

much thought it would be finished today.

Wednesday, June 14 - The night was rather bad, anguished by this instruction which did not take a step towards acquittal. Nine o'clock. I find myself in front of the cadi who is interrogating the witnesses of the death of Soleiman.

The first one deposits under the faith of the oath

– I was in the room next to the one occupied by Soleiman. He began to suffer so much around eleven o'clock in the evening that we rubbed him while reading the words of the Koran. He was given water from Zemzem (the miraculous spring of Mecca) to drink. We warned Soleiman Nana, with whom we were.

But by the time he got up and went to get a doctor, Soleiman was dead. Before he died I asked him what had made him sick. He simply replied :

– Emken Zeînab. Maybe Zeînab.

– Is that all ? They ask.

– That's it.

The second witness claims to have seen Soleiman take a red powder around 10 o'clock in the evening, dilute it in water and say by swallowing and joking :

– Maybe Zeinab loves another man and wants to get rid of me.

– What do you drink ?

– A remedy to purge myself.

At the moment of death and speaking to us, he murmured :

– It is surely Zeinab who kills me, and you will avange me and slit her throat.

The third witness, a kid about 15 years old, simply stated that his statement was the same as the previous witness, since they were together. He blushes, gets so confused that he can hardly say his name.

I challenge these testimonies, so different in such a short period of time : the hour of agony... I want us to finish, but the odious lawyer of the opposing party still wants a hearing to prove with doctors that it was my Kalmine that killed him.

The hearing is postponed to the next day; it is one o'clock; to come to terms with it, the cadi finally wants to start early and asks that we be there at eight o'clock.

Thursday, June 16 - I didn't sleep all night. I get up at 6 a.m. and wait. At 8:00 a.m., I beg a guard to take me to the court, he tells me to be ready, but to wait for a call. I try to hem a handkerchief, but I can barely hold my needle... I don't know what I'm doing anymore. I'm burning with impatience.

At 11 o'clock finally, we leave. I beg my boys to walk fast... I run. They get angry. It doesn't matter to me, I'm only interested in the final judgment. We arrive at the empty court. From the second day, the trial was held behind closed doors; an employee of the consulate having come to attend, the room was evacuated for good.

I ask if the doctors are coming. They are not here, I am afraid that they wanted to avoid a confrontation that was favorable to me in order to better accuse me.

I tremble with anguish. What is going to happen ?

After a few insignificant sentences, the cadi stands up and announces that the judgment is over... The doctors came and were questioned before my arrival.

ACQUITTED

I LOOK AT EVERYONE WITH ANGUISH. Questions are pressing on my lips. I want to know...

But the assistants don't seem to know whether I am acquitted or convicted. And looks are elusive when I try to read the truth on faces.

I urge the interpreter to get the decisive word from the cadi. The cadi is impassive and seems indifferent to my anger, to the tension I manifest. I insist on finally being a free prisoner. Some of them are. No one answers me anymore. I must leave. I return to my dungeon once again. I'm dripping, as one must be in the sweat of agony, my stockings and my veil, my hair itself is in revolution.

I write to the Emir, imploring his kindness, asking him to notify me of the result of the court's judgment. The consul comes to see me. He seems dismayed by this incomprehensible procedure. Usually several judgments are rendered in the morning... The length of the trial surprises him. His surprised and worried look disturbs me. I knew him so optimistic and so sure of himself until now !

– I may be sentenced to one or two years in prison, I said, horrified.

– I don't know, was his answer.

I am at the limit of my resistance. Even if I am sentenced to six months, I will commit suicide rather than stay in this dungeon. I can't take it anymore...

Friday 16 - No answer to my letter to the Emir. I am writing a second one. My despair reaches its peak. I repeat these words of Arab supplication : "O God, do not give to man all that he can suffer".

I am again summoned before the cadi.

I have to swear in Arabic. As I don't know these formulas, I repeat them after my interpreter.

Solemnly, with my hand on the Koran, I pronounce the ritual and sacred syllables.

– Khalas ! (finished), finally drops the cadi.

– Thank you, thank you, do you allow me to go directly to the consulate ?

– Go back to the prison, he replies coldly.

– No, no, now it's impossible, you said it's over, you're the judge, tell me what you think, what you decide. Everything depends on you. I would rather you have me killed, but finish it. Cut it out, judge, I won't leave until you answer me. I can no longer contemplate you still so impassive. Speak and answer.

– Only Allah knows the truth ! He will decide.

– You are Allah for me, you only have a word to say to decide my fate.

Smiles on faces, but the cadi wants to leave. I throw myself on him, the guards are ordered to take me away. I roll on the floor, the interpreters tell me that they have to deliberate, that they will call me back in fifteen minutes. I regain courage, I leave, the soldiers who are supervising me think that I'm going to be free.

Alas ! the quarter of an hour passes, I am not called back. I found out later that the interpreters, disturbed, embarrassed in front of a mad woman, had invented this quarter of an hour of waiting to cheer me up.

Sunday, June 18 - I am still waiting for someone to signify life or death to me. This waiting makes me sick. I think I am on the verge of the grave. My sadness is insurmountable. I feel that the end is near, but I no longer dare to hope for freedom.

Monday, June 19 - Still nothing; the consul brings me newspapers for the first time. Marise Hilsz went to Paris-Saigon-Tokyo and back. I feel like I was buried alive for 75 days. I taste the pleasantness of waking up without having the right to let myself go because I don't yet know what my destiny will be.

I always ask the consul if he sees in the baccalaureate exams the name of my son who was supposed to appear at the beginning of the month. I think that the High Commission of Beirut would have telegraphed him this news to please me. But on all sides, silence, ignorance...

Tuesday, June 20 - Still without news, the wait undermines and annihilates me.

Wednesday, June 21 - I was told that the king leaves for the desert where Er Riad, its capital, is located.

When he leaves Mecca, a big suite follows him 100 or 200 kilometers away in the arid sands. The cadi, of course, moves with the retinue of the sovereign. Will I have the strength to wait any longer ?

Thursday, June 22 - I sit on my bed all day without doing anything. Life abandons me. The consul comes to see me, he looks very down and doesn't talk about leaving anymore. Yet Jaber Effendi tells me that the papers from Mecca may arrive on Saturday, because it seems that my trial had been sent to Mecca to the cadi of cadis.

Saturday June 24 - The consul is ill. He sends me a member of the consulate to give me courage and to tell me that the solution is imminent.

Sunday - I hear a very young man being beatten in the next room. He is howling in pain. I try to intervene with the guards through the bars. They burst out laughing.

Monday, June 26 - At noon, the director of police calls me into his office. It is the first time and I hardly know him. Two days after my arrest, Saïd Bey, who had a reputation for violence and brutality, was moved to avoid serious incidents. I am tired of these eternal interrogations that lead to nothing.

The director makes me sit next to him. He seems to be telling me a little story. I can only understand one word "Baria" (innocent).

– Of course I am.

– It was the cadi who said so.

– Ah ! so much the better, but then...

He floods me with a flood of sentences. I realize this very badly and I don't dare to understand. I understand Jaber Effendi much better when he speaks to me. We call him, he explains to me.

– Don't you understand that you are "out", free !

– Free, ah ! I understand this word... free.

I take the Director's hand in my own two hands,

I hold it tight, I thank him, I tell him that he is beautiful, good, nice. I jump, I tap on the shoulder of all the soldiers who watch the scene without flinching.

I shout to them : Out... out... free... free ! Can I leave ?

The police chief nods his head in an affirmative sign with a good smile.

I run up to the small ladder, I turn around and laugh, I say hello to everyone.

Finally, Jaber Effendi, more serious and cold than ever, intervenes. In a rogue, hard tone, he calls out to me :

– Zeinab, are you crazy ?

"Maloum". Naturally. Yes, yes, crazy with joy. And, I set off in a frantic race, without returning in my dungeon, I run through the stairs, the policemen and the streets... to the French consulate.

THE LIFE-SAVING STOP

RUNNING MADLY IN THE STREETS, SOMETIMES dark, sometimes cluttered with sunlight, without escort and without seeing anything, I arrive at the Legation of France.

The consul greets me with a sensitive emotion. He is also astonished to see me suddenly released without a final judgment.

He asks me with curiosity :

– But how did it happen ? What did they tell you ?

Breathless, trembling with joy, I spout out a flood of words among which Mr. M... must try to restore reality.

– The cadi of the cadis recognized my innocence. Then he let me know through the director of police that I could leave my dungeon. And here I am.

– But with which documents related to the case ?

– None. I was told : "You are free. I don't know either if I am condemned to pay a ransom, or if I should return to Soleiman's family the price he supposedly bought me for. Nor do I know if I am a prisoner in Djeddah or if I am definitively freed.

I will wait for the official notification. Let's wait. The day passes for me in joy. Alone, I know at this moment how to appreciate the return to freedom and civilization. I have lived death as much as it is possible to a living being. Also, I touch all things as if I had just returned from the beyond.

The smallest realities fill me with happiness. A thousand ideas cross my mind : I would like to take away from the souks a lot of memories, I would like to go back and thank my dear Sett Kébir.

The consul wants to avoid any incident and asks me not to go out in the souks. We only go, in the evening, to walk by the sea.

I am unveiled, thinking that no Arab will recognize me. But as I pass my prison, I make great gestures of friendship to my guards. It is in vain that they want to stop my demonstrations, because here they are dangerous and unseemly acts. A little more discretion would be in better taste, but I don't have the strength to hold back the happy fever that fills me.

However, I cannot remain in this strange situation of a woman who yesterday was under a capital charge and who does not know whether she is on provisional release or not. The consul calls the Emir of Djeddah on the phone to know the text of the judgment rendered.

And I finally found out about my own adventure.

There are, at the consulate, a lot of newspapers concerning my case. What is not my surprise in reading the Syrian and Egyptian periodicals which abound in hypotheses full of fantasy ! The French, English, Italian, German, American and even Estonian press announced my death...

For some, it was hanging, for others, classic stoning.

L'Orient, a Beirut newspaper (which was later the only one that did not retract its slander and which I could not prosecute, as the French government kept me in Paris and the time limit for prosecuting the press was three months), however, holds my attention, because it seems to give the best explanation for this inexplicable adventure summarized in these few lines :

It seems that the facts could plausibly be established as follows :

"It is said that the Wahhabit police killed the meharist in order to put the blame for this crime on the daring foreign spy and then legally get rid of her."

The next day, in the evening, when I suggested the walk that had done me so much good the day before, a member of the consulate recounts that he had heard in town that the president of the Virtue Commission had ordered two zealots to stand in front of the consulate door to strick out at Zeinab with their "hassa" (whip) if she tried to come out unveiled.

To ensure compliance with all religious rules, the leaders of Wahhabism had recourse, and this, from the very beginning, to spies of the kind of the sycophants of Greek history, and the famous explorer Palgrave tells in his journey to the center of Arabia (around 1860) that he had to deal with this kind of spies that he called "zealots".

Today these "zealots" are represented by the Virtue Commission, composed of officials charged with the task of identifying any infraction of the related law and referring any offender directly to the cadi.

Two European women who had gone bare arms into the souks of Djeddah were arrested and taken to the police, but their husbands being diplomats, they were released.

The consul decides to be cautious and to renounce to too many walks.

The next day, at breakfast time, I hear that my judgment is published in the newspaper of Mecca. Here is the translation :

"JUDGMENT IN THE SOLEIMAN DIKMARI CASE :

Oum Elquora of 7 Rabbia 1352.

The cadi of the court of first instance in Djeddah has just handed down its judgment in the case of the heirs of Soleiman Dikmari against Zeînab bent Maksime. This judgment was submitted for appeal to the cadi of the cadis who confirmed it.

The trial of the accused took place in Djeddah on 23 Safar. The investigation, the appearance of witnesses, and judicial formalities required several hearings. The cadi's judgment was recorded on a lengthy document that reportedly filled out several sheets of this journal. We will simply reproduce the extract from the paragraph containing the decision. The cadi, having examined the main charge as well as the secondary issues that have been grafted onto it, rendered the following separate judgments in each of these cases :

1 - By virtue of the written acts emanating from the competent services of the place of marriage, the validity of this marriage between the accused and the victim has been established.

2 - The plaintiff was unable to establish the guilt of the interested party and could only give certain statements supposedly given by the victim, who was in agony, and according to which he accused his wife;

Given the lack of evidence on one hand, and, on the other hand, the cadi having taken into consideration the disagreement then existing between the two spouses;

Fearing, therefore, that the victim had wanted revenge on his wife, and for other legal reasons set out in the act, the cadi issued a judgment acquitting her of the charge of poisoning her husband, and halting all proceedings against her by the heirs.

3 - With regard to the succession, the cadi issued a judgment disinheriting the accused.

4 - He sentenced the defendant to a disgraceful sentence, as it was established that she had been with a stranger,

Since the period of detention of the accused corresponds to the period provided for in the judgment, the accused was released. "

Officially acquitted, I am therefore free. All that remains for me to do is to think about the departure. I have only one idea, to return to Syria as soon as possible.

The consul therefore instructs one of his secretaries to complete the necessary formalities to obtain my Nedjien passport from S. M. Ibn Saud. Everything now seemed to work out for the best, I was only thinking of my return to Palmyra, to see Pierre, my husband, my children, my friends, when, under the influence of an inexplicable turn of events, the whole consulate gathered for dinner began to advise me to leave for France instead, avoiding passing through Syria, for fear of disturbances that my return could provoke among the Arabs, after this tragic attempt at a muslim marriage.

First of all, I don't attach any importance to all this advice. I repeat to everyone that I have nothing to do in France, while everything awaits me in Syria, and the evenings are spent playing bridge and poker with our neighbor the delegate of the Iraqi legation, Guelani Bey.

I can't imagine then what awaits me. Of course, it is not a death sentence, but it is a kind of civil death, without any understandable motive and which can only be explained by the fear that sometimes fills the soul of the little civil servants who make the law in the administration. Law that is always summed up in the formula : "Above all, no drama".

THIS IS NOT THE END

I HAD RETIRED TO MY ROOM AT AROUND one o'clock and was already asleep, when I was woken up, about two hours later, by someone knocking on my door.

– But who is there ?

– It's me, answered the consul. Please be so kind as to follow me into the next room. I have a few words to say to you.

I jump out of bed in a hurry. What can he want from me at this hour ?

I have just been taught an unworthy and awful, absurd and crazy decision. For, with all possible restraint, the consul, who understood how much trouble it would cause me, confided to me that a telegram from Beirut, in response to the one which inform them of my release, orders Mr. M... to stamp my passport exclusively for France, without authorization to disembark in Syria.

And the High Commissioner adds that I have lost my French nationality.

The consul knew this during the dinner, but he wanted to tell me only after the guests had left, anticipating my grief and my reactions. He knows how happy I was to return to my family after a separation that was almost final. But we have to give it up, because in two days the boat will be here.

However, all may not be lost. Two days still allow to exchange dispatches. Mr. M... seing my despair, promises to insist once again to the High Commissioner, explaining that after the moral misery I have just suffered and from which I have barely escaped, I cannot be forced to accept the financial catastrophe that will be the expulsion from Palmyra, where my family, my property, my home and where my business await me.

I go back to my room, bending under this new and   desperate ordeal.

My enemies in Syria, against whom I had already fought so hard, took advantage of my absence to harm me, and then used my terrible adventure to convince the High Commissioner that I was becoming unwanted. In fact, after twenty-four hours, Beirut refused my request. Of course, this is supposedly out of consideration and kindness, in order to save me from the terrible dangers I would face on my way back to Syria.

I'm perfectly assured that nothing will get to me.

I can even add that, if there were demonstrations against me, they would be provoked by the suborders of the High Commission. If even I were murdered, it would be at their instigation and I know who...

However, my situation is complicated by the fact that the sovereign Nedjien, in turn, answers every day about my passport : tomorrow, "bokra, bokra".

Finally, after eight days, Ibn Saud's Minister of Foreign Affairs arrives with this annoying and final answer :

– The Zeinab woman has caused us enough trouble, so let her go. But we don't want to give her a Nedjien passport.

So, what to do ? Nothing else now but to have my old passport for France stamped.

The next boat leaves Djeddah tomorrow. Alas ! my departure is still postponed, under the pretext that the Great Torturer of Mecca will embark tomorrow for Suez. They fear putting me in contact with this torturer who, in short, bitterly regrets not having had the pleasure of torturing me. It seems that he has some genius finds in this field.

However, bridge and poker evenings continue at the consulate. It is overwhelmingly hot. One sponges the forehead with a handkerchief that is always wet. On the other hand one would like to fan out. And the glasses of whisky served to us by our host are really well received.

There's a mischief that is becoming classic. Tired people are offered a "Kalmine pill". We laugh... But the Kalmine itself is now frightening.

Finally, it was decided that, in eight days, I would take the liner.

And then, on the morning of the departure, we hear again that the Great Torturer, whom we thought already far away, will still be there, at my side... It is too late to delay again.

Never mind ! We will see what happens.

The consul bids me a simple and laconic farewell. He knows how much admiration, gratitude and affection I will keep for him all my life.

We leave the consulate by car, but near the pier, an agitated and hateful crowd is held back by armed policemen, and they look at me ferociously. I pass between this double hedge, under my veil. The French flag must be hoisted on the launch to prevent fanatics who have entered the water from capsizing the boat.

The ship that carries me away is English : the Taïf. All the staff of the consulate, who accompany me, explain to the commander the delicacy of my situation. There are Nedjians on board, and I am told to stay locked up in my cabin. It is necessary to avoid incidents that could lead to my disembarking in the two ports of the Hedjaz where we call : Ouedj and Yambo.

There, no one would have the power to serve me. But I think we're exaggerating. The boat is leaving. From the porthole, I watch Djeddah moving away, I climb on the deck.

I find the delegate from Iraq, a charming man, who takes me under his protection. He advises me to stay in my cabin at the ports of call; if there is any danger, he warns me.

We decide to have our meals together, conversing about a thousand things that are familiar to us, and enter the dining room. As soon as we enter, the famous Great Torturer of Mecca appears : Maadi bey.

He is a mature man in appearance, although he is only forty years old, he will tell me later. He appears stiff, thin, dry, with sharp eyes and unquestionable prestige. When he sees me, he has a step back.

I feel a hesitation in this terrible man, and I call out to him brutally :

– Are you ashamed to sit next to a woman coming out of prison ?

He decides to articulate slowly :

– No, certainly ! and, regaining his firmness, he takes a chair and sits down beside me, confiding to me :

"I am all the less ashamed to sit next to you, Zeinab, because the government never believed you were guilty."

Afterwards, I had long discussions with him. We discuss my business, and this man, whose profession is hideous, has strange tastes of fairness. When one thinks, however, that his only concern is to make those he tortures suffer and to bring to death only after as much suffering as possible, one feels cold to the soul.

What I know of his exploits is atrocious. He tells me about them himself. Not long ago he tortured three men, who were executed three days before my release, and this is how it was done :

The first one was whipped until all the skin was torn off. It was then sprinkled with fresh water to revive the burn, then he was plunged up to his chin into a pit filled with human waste...

The second, locked in a black dungeon, heard in the next room the iron bars blushing and boiling water from a boiler. Suddenly, in the darkness, several men jumped on their victim with red irons, etc., and the unfortunate man confessed what he had refused to recognize before.

The third was of noble race, the Emir of Oneiza's own cousin. So it was Maadi bey himself who tortured him. The Great Torturer took the man out of the city and kept him for five days without food or drink. He then gave him all the food he wanted, covered with salt, and water refreshed in a guerba (goatskin wineskin). Beforehand, the manly limb is tied to him and the other orifices are obstructed. After hours of suffering the poor man says he will confess. The ties are undone, but he has nothing to say. The torture is repeated and he confesses, perhaps judging death preferable. In Djeddah, I am told that an elderly man caught the lover of his young wife leaving his house. The young woman denied the meeting and the jealous old man instructed slaves to announce the visit of her lover for the next day. At the appointed hour, the happy and adorned woman waits, when two men enter, her husband, and then... another being, but who no longer has a human face. On one bloody face the eyes, the teeth, everything else is gnawed away, stripped of flesh.

For two days his head, locked in a wooden cage, has been tortured by a rat. In order to attract this hungry beast beforehand, the cheeks, nose, forehead, and lips have been coated with fat, and the wild beast devoured them.

The young woman faints, the man dies shortly afterwards.

Maadi bey is still here, sitting next to me. This man, who would have liked to increase my agony of all tortures, expresses himself on everything with delicacy and seems to forget his monstrous profession.

He is not a simple executioner, a beheader or a hangman. He is a "torturer", a specialist in human suffering, a sort of psychologist who is concerned about the sensitivity of his fellow human beings. He is constantly looking for the most subtle ways to create and revive pain beyond measure...

According to him, in Soleiman's death, there is a culprit and the investigation was badly carried out, following only one lead : mine.

– Soleiman, Maadi bey resumes, would he have committed suicide at the sight of your coldness and disdain ?

I dissuade him from this big mistake.

Soleiman boasted everywhere about his brilliant marriage, has he been the victim of a thief ?

All the checks were found on him, but this fiduciary currency is misunderstood by the indigenous people of the Hedjaz. What other hypotheses ?

I do believe that Maadi bey would be able to provide some that would be more in line with the truth. But he is also a diplomat...

On the last day, he regretted that I didn't have a daughter because, he said, he would marry her. I look at his white hair with a smile.

He understands and apologizes for this apparent old age which is the result of the hard life he leads...

The rest of the crossing went without incident. Naser bey, the Iraqi delegate, holds the most interesting conversations with me. He tells me that he is a descendant of the "Hashemites" (Mohamed's family) and a former chief of protocol for Emir Faisal, King of Iraq. He knows, of course, all the arab and muslim customs, and explains to me in detail the formalities that I have to accomplish with the brothers of Soleiman. As long as this question is not settled, I and those of my blood, that is, my sons, will be in danger of death. He promises to go and explain it, when he passes through Beirut, to Mr. Ponsot, High Commissioner, since I will not be able to do it myself. He also told me that the Arab always makes an ennemy pay, in the case of assassination, the "dia", the blood tax.

The protocol is as follows :

As soon as I return to Palmyra, I will have to go to the brothers of Soleiman, accompanied by an armed escort, because then I will be in danger.

When I arrive at their house, they will offer me coffee that I will drink and say a few words, neither too kind nor too cold; the name Soleiman should not be pronounced.

Then I will greet them and leave. They in turn will pay me back this visit, will refuse my tea, will perhaps ask me about Soleiman. After that, I will choose two Arab friends to discuss with two representatives of the family of the deceased. These emissaries will agree on the compensation I owe them; guilty or innocent, it doesn't matter, the "dia" must be paid. This settlement will completely end the whole affair.

We finally arrive in Suez; on the quay, my husband is waiting for me and, ironically, welcomes me with these words :

– You must be very tired, here. And he pulls a Kalmine tablet from his pocket...

I call Naser bey and Maadi bey and show them the famous little box, greeted by a general burst of laughter.

– Unbelievable ! they exclaim.

CONCLUSION

I HAD FOUND OUT AT DJEDDAH THAT the High Commissioner had intervened with the English Government to allow me to spend five days in Palestine to see my son. Why five days, since I have a passport for Palestine valid for one year ?

It is probably the unfavourable information from the French government that earned me this extraordinary measure; in fact, when I arrived at the border of Kantara *(1)*, the one-year residence permit was barred on my passport and replaced by the words "five days". I am trying to find out from my husband what the High Commissioner's reasons are for preventing me from returning to Syria.

He told me that he feared demonstrations against me, which would disrupt public order. Hadn't one insinuated, in fact, to find an explanation for the fact that I often share the life of the Bedouins in the desert, that I wanted to be proclaimed queen of the Bedouins ? Poor civil servants and politicians, who see everyone in their own image and cannot even believe in a simple friendship with indigenous tribes without imagining absurd ambitions.

As soon as I landed in Haifa, I wrote a letter to the High Commissioner, telling him that I find unacceptable the measure taken against me, and that it is lamentable to note that after ten

(1) Place where passports for Palestine are stamped.

years of politics in Syria, they are afraid of a simple woman and her Arab friendships. What was the point of helping me to save myself, only to overwhelm me further ? I consider that everything is the fault of the French authorities in Syria, which probably reported me as a spy to Sheikh Abdel Raouf, consul of the Nedj in Damascus. I would like to make it clear that I cannot prove this accusation, but it seems certain that my horrible enemies in the Damascus Legation, who have long wanted me to leave, will have given the Nedj consul the worst information about me. This sheik, being an official representative, was only able to address himself to other official personalities, which explains the importance he attached to this information, which he believed it was his duty to transmit to his king.

It is moreover certain that it was related to

Mr. Véber, interim delegate, (known by his falsity) for wanting only him as a witness at my wedding.

Here are some newspaper articles reporting the information obtained on my account by Sheikh Abdel Raouf. It is only natural, after such calumnies, that the king had me arrested in the Red Sea.

Article published in May 1933, in L'Orient, the French daily newspaper in Beirut :

" TRAGIC EPILOGUE"

"The Countess d'Andurain was reportedly hanged yesterday in Mecca.

A dispatch arrived from Mecca on Wednesday morning, laconically announcing that the Countess of Andurain, having been summarily tried yesterday morning, Tuesday, and sentenced to death, was hanged immediately.

An investigation allows us to give details on this case.

The Countess d'Andurain, a French woman, came to Dramas two months ago and presented herself, in the company of a muslim meharist, to Sheik Abdel Raouf, consul of the Nedj-Hedjaz in the Syrian capital.

The countess asked the consul to contract marriage with the meharist and to register this marriage at the Chancellery in order to obtain a regular passport. The consul asked the countess to return the next day. In the meantime Sheikh Raouf was conducting an investigation. The next day, the consul told the Countess that he was very sorry that he could not give a favorable response to her request.

Mrs d'Andurain did not admit defeat. She went to Palestine, and found a more accommodating consul in Jaffa who satisfied all her desires.

Having dismissed the Countess, Sheikh Abdel, Raouf, as one might think, immediately addressed a long rapport to the Sultan of Nedj-Hedjaz, Ibn El Saud, to tell him about the strange request he had received from the Countess.

Ibn El Saud was therefore alerted.

Ten days ago the news from Mecca announced that the Countess' second hand husband had been found poisoned, that the Countess had been arrested because a violent poison had been discovered on her, enclosed in a bag...

The telegram announcing the summary judgment and the execution of the

212

Countess d'Andurain thus appears as the painful epilogue of an adventurous journey.

Did the Countess really, as some relationships indicate, kill her companion ? The thing seems doubtful.

From the circumstances we have just reported on this odyssey, it seems that the facts could probably be re-established as follows : The meharist was allegedly killed by Wahhabi police in order to put the blame of the crime to the foreigner and then legally dispose of it.

Article of May 12, 1933 in the East :

"THE TRAGIC ODYSSEY OF THE COUNTESS D'ANDURAIN."

"We reported yesterday, according to a private telegram from Mecca, which had been very difficult to decipher, having been written, as one thinks, in conventional language, that the Countess d'Andurain, convinced that she had poisoned her second hand husband, a Bedouin, would have been summarily judged and executed immediately.

No official confirmation of the terrible news has yet been received.

The information reproduced yesterday by the East has caused a deep and painful impression in all circles, and we still want to wish that the telegram from Mecca was wrong.

Yesterday, we were able to gather some new information that suggested that the author of the dispatch from Mecca only reported a rumor, which circulated in the capital of Islam".

"NEW DETAILS"

"We have information that the tragedy, if there was a tragedy, must have taken place in Djeddah and not in Mecca.

As is well known, Wahhabi law prohibits any Christian who embraces islamism from traveling to Mecca until one year after conversion.

Was the Countess d'Andurain unaware of this detail, did she hasten her visit to the "Kaaba" for reasons we do not know ?

Still, the traveller had to stop at Djeddah, and that it was there that her fictitious husband, the Bedouin, was found dead.

We can add that the corpse of the individual was sent to Egypt for autopsy and that the response of the experts of the Egyptian laboratory did not have the material time to arrive in Djeddah, unless it was wired, which seems doubtful... and probable at the same time.

Doubtful, because a medical report of such a high severity requires development. Likely if the Wahhabi authority, whose tendencies are known, wanted, because of the personality of the victim, to put the world in front of an accommodating fact and prevent any diplomatic intervention.

Ibn Saud's people can rightly be suspected.

There are some disturbing facts against them

1° First of all, the warning of the consul of the Nedj-Hijaz in Damascus, who warned, rightly or wrongly, of the arrival of an "informer" carrying a poison, and accompanied by a fictitious husband;

2° The sudden departure of the consul from Damascus, and his embarkation for Egypt on the eve of the execution of the "Frenchwoman".

3° The Wahabite authorities of Djeddah, instead of expelling the Countess, kept her in this city and imposed her to stay there under the pretext of the application of the one year period provided by the law.

In any case, in the presence of so much contradictory informations, all these hypotheses can only be accepted with the most express reservations.

The only certain fact is that the Countess D'andurain, accused of poisoning her fictitious husband, was incarcerated in Djeddah on April 21 and has not been released.

Let us recall, for those who did not know it, that the Count and Countess D'andurain have been established for five years in Palmyra, where they acquired the property of the Hotel Zenobia, which has since become the luxurious desert palace of worldwide reputation.

The countess D'andurain is for the Bedouins the castelaine of Palmyra: a kind of new Zenobia.

Mrs D'andurain is known throughout the Syrian desert, which she travels continuously, buying cattle and lending money.

To facilitate her travel, she recently obtained an air pilot's license, but the government did not grant her permission to have a private plane".

This is the kind of articles, along with many others, very slanderous, that the press has spread about me. Personally, I do not consider that I have anything to reproach myself for, and that I simply wanted to make an exploration which, with more liberal compatriots, would not have caused me any difficulty.

I would have crossed a country that no European has yet set foot in; without the odious machinations of which I was a victim, the adventure would have been a complete success, I would have divorced Soleiman on my return, and few people would have known this marriage of cir- constancy. But these bourgeois and petty minds, who hated me, could not believe that the love of fantasy and the unexpected could make me risk my life, contract a fictitious marriage, etc., an incorrigible French routine.

As soon as I arrived at the consulate, I tried to form a precise opinion on the way things had happened and on the unknown influences that may have played a role, in this adventure that almost cost me my life.

I released from the jumble of sensational, slanderous and false news that had been published by the press the only probable explanation of the mystery of Soleiman's death and, by these very facts, of the failure of my project.

Here, in a few words, is the hypothesis that I have definitively rallied to :

The king of the Nedj, Ibn Saud, having received worrying information about my so-called activity as a French-English spy, had to put everything at stake to stop me as soon as I landed in Djeddah. Legally, however, I was perfectly in order, as a muslim and a Nedjian, and, on the other hand, he probably feared, by making me disappear in the desert, that he would attract diplomatic complications from the countries of which I was supposed to be the agent. It was much simpler to suppress Soleiman and to accuse me of his death, with the help of the false testimonies of those who supposedly assisted the dying man. We know that, according to Koranic law, the word of the dying man is authoritative and leads to condemnation without judgment.

I must add that the French delegate, Mr. Maigret, never believed this version, although I tried to show him the disturbing coincidences between this hypothesis and the facts as they happened. On my arrival in Paris I also had a conversation on this subject with Si Kaddour ben Gabrit, a personal friend of King Ibn Saud who refused to admit such a machination on the part of His Majesty.

They have their opinion, I have mine.

Given all these facts, it remains to explain the attitude of the French Government which, although my total innocence has been recognized, since I was acquitted for lack of a single piece of evidence and the only charge against me was based on the words of the dying man (were they pronounced ?), refuses to let me return to Syria and, after forcing me to return to France, condemns me to live in Paris, while all my interests are in the East. The Government denies me my French nationality, which all the lawyers are unanimous in finding illegal. According to the law, there are two ways to lose the French nationality. The first, by renouncing it through an official document at the time of marriage with a foreigner, a document that does not exist, since I did not sign anything of this kind. The other, by electing to live abroad with her husband : since my marriage to Soleiman, I have only lived in the harem where I was sequestered, and the prison where I was sentenced to death. Now the Foreign Affairs have the impudence to consider this stay as an election of domicile. It is astonishing that they do not add that I chose it with joy.

Currently, I am a prisoner in Paris, without nationality since the king did not want to give me Nedjian papers and the French government refuses to give me any official documents such as a passport, certificate of residence, etc..

My notary, Mr Champetier de Ribes, even refused to legalize my maiden name, one of which a woman always has the right to use.

I have been waiting for a year from the Minister of Finance in Damascus for the payment of an annuity that the Government is making to the Bedouins and which, as a result of a judgment, is reversible on my head, to reimburse me for the sums I had lent to Sheikh Naouf, of the Hadidin tribe. The Minister of Finance asked for a certificate proving that I was alive, since the newspapers had announced my death.

The Foreign Affairs and the Syrian Office, consulted, refused me a certificate of domicile under a pretext that it was not within their competence.

Am I condemned to live all my life as an outlaw ? and why ?

No one can reproach me anything, officially, because I have done nothing shameful or illegal.

And yet, part of my family, caught in the wave of shyness, cowardice, fear of what will be said that is sweeping France at the moment, thought of having me hospitalized. My closest relative spoke to Garat, the deputy mayor of Bayonne, currently living at Villa Chalgrin (prison), who had the audacity to ask for my expulsion from France in a letter I read, addressed to the district attorney of Bayonne.

Could there be a more striking example of the smallness and pettiness, the low cowardice of those who follow the routine of a life mapped out the day they were born, and their total lack of understanding of fantasy and independence ?

It's still quite fun to know how you were cried over. I don't think anyone more than me, who is so keen to know what people really think, even if it is the worst, could have been more joyful than by the letters of condolence to my husband, sons, brother, etc.

Also, with what delights I became aware of these last expressions of affection that I was not destined to see.

LETTER FROM A FIRST COUSIN TO MY BROTHER :

"Florence, June 5, 1933.

My poor Pitt (1),

I just found out, by a letter, the horrible news. I am devastated, deeply moved. I think of your pain and hasten to come to you to express my most painful condolences; my deepest sympathy. The unfortunate woman has hard atoned for a life of carelessness and levity. I don't dare to write to Pio (2), poor kid, I pity him with all my soul as well as little Jacques (3). May God help them and support them in this harsh ordeal. I am with you with all my heart...".

Carelessness, levity : because my life is not classically bourgeois, it is fatally misjudged by these people with an average mind...

After these observations, is it any wonder that I want to live in the desert or in the sea, far from the rot of horrible civilization ?

March 9, 1934.
Marga D'ANDURAIN
Prisoner in Paris.

(1) Pitt, my brother.
(2) Pio, my eldest son,
(3) Jacques, my youngest son.

BIOGRAPHY

To relate the life of Marga d'Andurain and to give a plausible picture of it, it is necessary to rely on her autobiographical book, "Passport Husband", written in 1934 and published one year before her death, in 1947, and to compare it with some articles of the time, as well as the memoirs of her son Jacques, published in 2007.

Childhood and youth

Marguerite "Marga" Clérisse was born on May 29, 1893 in the Basque Country into an upper middle-class family. Her father, Maxime Clérisse, was a magistrate at the court of Bayonne, and her mother, Marie Diriart, had no profession. Marguerite also had a brother nicknamed "Pitt" and a sister, Mathilde. Her traditionalist family had given her a Catholic education and had sent her to Spain for her schooling. She had a very classical childhood, despite a difficult and voluble character. In his book, "An odd mother", Marga's son, Jacques d'Andurain, describes his grand parents as nostalgic for the monarchy and obsessed with finding noble alliances for their children. In spite of all this and in spite of an independence of spirit which one found to her *a posteriori* and of which she herself undoubtedly amplified the value at justifying ends, she had the conventional life of a young girl from a good family in the provincial France of the beginning of the 20th century.

Even if Marga, in her auto-biography, likes to describe herself as an adventuress, a revolutionary, fighting with force against the supposed small-mindedness, pettiness and bigotry of her native environment, far from being in rupture with the family creed, Marga, like her husband, turns out to have shared all her life, the convictions and choices of her parents. A member of the monarchist and anti-Dreyfus political movement "Action Française", obsessed with the aristocracy that she considered her "world", assailing her children with injunctions to associate with "good people", despising people who were not of her rank, etc. In terms of social ambitions, the daughter of Maxime and Marie Clérisse behaved like a perfect upstart. An upstart, not a revolutionary. She did not dream of destroying the world of the powerful, she wanted to be in it, that's different.

In 1909, Marga met one of her distant cousins, Pierre d'Andurain, 12 years her senior. Their marriage was celebrated on February 13, 1911. Her father, Maxime Clérisse, had accepted the union with reluctance, because if the particle of the name was acquired, he did not appreciate the fact that his future son-in-law was still "without profession". Marga was going to discover that this was not a passing fancy but a way of life. For if he had many qualities - tall, handsome, affable, passionate about horseback riding - Pierre was reluctant to work. To make the father accept this marriage, Marga and Pierre, with the complicity of Marga's mother, in a hurry to marry her daughter, assured Maxime Clérisse that a job in insurance was promised to the future groom by a friend, when he returned from his honeymoon. The couple started out in life relying on the generosity of their families for a while, but very soon they had to face the facts: they had to find a way to finance a life "worthy of their rank" without having to work.

The problem was that she needed a fortune that she did not have and that neither she, nor her husband Pierre d'Andurain, were able to obtain by conventional means. For if the d'Andurains came from the Basque nobility, they were neither titled nor wealthy. As Jacques d'Andurain writes in his memoirs: "My father had no fortune, no hopes. His deceased father, a cavalry officer, had left so little (...) he had neither a situation, nor a vocation, nor any dream of a productive activity of money".

Wanderings and World War I

Their honeymoon, which was supposed to last a few weeks in Spain, finally dragged on to Morocco and then Algeria; their first son, Jean-Pierre, was born there on December 4, 1911. But how to face the return home and the consequences of the deception ? There was no job waiting for Pierre d'Audurain in France.

The couple lived on the income from Marga's marriage dowry. The dowry system was a system to give a dowry to his daughter, without the husband being able to squander it. The newlyweds could only receive the dowry annuity offering a 3 to 5% return.

But this income is not enough to finance the idle life that the young couple dreams of leading. Financial difficulties made them return to France.

Quickly, the couple wishes to leave again. Argentina, land of Eldorado for all Basques at the time, was chosen as the destination where the young couple intended to breed horses. Noble work par excellence, the only one that Pierre d'Andurain considered worthy of him. Determined to take the destiny of his family into his own hands, he asked for family support one last time. The families financed the trip. Pierre left alone in the summer of 1912 before being joined by his young wife and their son. They stayed for 2 years.

The Sarajevo bombing and the outbreak of World War I put an end to their Argentine dream. An Argentine dream that had never really taken off. The couple being bad managers, the business had quickly collapsed.

Pierre wished to return to fight. But the young lieutenant had disci -

pline problems. One day, he refused his colonel's orders and had a violent altercation with him to the point where he slapped him. Thanks to his connections, he avoided the council of war, and was sent back to the Basque Country where he finished the war as a border guard. He was thus able to attend the birth of his second son, Jacques, born on November 26, 1916.

The Great War ended quietly without the family understanding that the "Belle Epoque" was behind them. The world had changed, the cards had been reshuffled. The "end of the rentiers" was going to force them more than ever to invent their life in a more enchanting place. The couple moved to Paris where they hoped to rub shoulders with the beautiful world. The children stayed with the family in the Basque country. But the fall of the income after the First World War causes the impoverishment of the family. Marga decides to work.

However, she understood that in "her world", work, especially for women, remained a sign of decadence. It was only allowed if it could be considered a hobby. So she chose interior design, buying and selling apartments that she had transformed. Then, she developed the production of artificial pearls under the brand *Arga*. With the complicity of a chemist cousin, they create artificial pearls that perfectly imitate the real ones. The fake pearl scam worked, and the customers were delighted.

The fake pearls business could have brought in a lot of money, but the d'Audurains were not diligent, and they were bad managers. Pierre cared about what people thought. The noble name of the d'Andurains was effective, but it was not enough to give the change to the Parisian high society. One always needs more money. One must impress. It was lost in advance.

In 1925, Marga inherits from her father. The funds are important. She liquidated the pearl company and sold the Parisian apartment. The couple fled to Egypt.

But in the Middle East, Marga wants to be part of the expatriate high society. She is adamant : she needs a title. So Marga spent weeks searching the family tree of the d'Andurains for hypothetical ancestors who could provide them with the much-desired grail. All in vain.

If the title of nobility does not exist, then it must be invented ! That's how Marga the commoner gave herself the title of Viscountess of Andurain. The business cards are printed. In Egypt, it will be "Viscount and Viscountess Pierre and Marga d'Andurain". There, nobody knew them and nobody would question this title.

Destination: the Orient

Marga arrived in Egypt, where, adorned with her title of "viscountess" she immediately became part of the British community in Cairo. She opened the *Mary Stuart* beauty Institute to receive rich Egyptian and European women. Business was booming. But Pierre is bored.

Two years later, accompanied by two English friends including Major Sinclair, she made a trip to the East (Jerusalem, the Dead Sea) and discovered the ruins of Palmyra in Syria. It was love at first sight, so much so that she immediately decided to move there with her family. They stayed there for 9 years, from 1927 to 1936. She also took Major Sinclair as her lover.

Pierre would be able to indulge his passion for horses, while she would manage (and then buy in 1930 for 150,000 francs at the time) the Kettaneh Hotel, renamed Zenobia Hotel. But as soon as they settled in, trouble was already brewing. Refusing to take into account the rivalry between the French and the British in the region, Marga had not understood how much her arrival on the arm of a British officer - her lover - could have damaged her image and fueled suspicions of espionage among the soldiers of the Palmyra post. Was this exaggerated ? No, especially if one takes into account the context of the post-war period where the myth of the female spy had largely fuelled the popular chronicles. Ignoring these accusations, she settled into the position of the new queen of Palmyra, welcoming the few tourists and distinguished guests who passed through the desert city, while partly governing the life of the Arab village where she found her employees.

But the couple may have had another reason to settle in Palmyra. As Jacques d'Andurain recounts in his memoirs, since their arrival in Middle East, the couple had been taking drugs. She, cocaine, he, opium. Palmyra is a crossroads where caravans from Turkey and Persia, two drug-producing regions, meet.

The couple's drug addiction is expensive, especially since the Zenobia Hotel, located in the middle of the desert, does not bring in fortunes. The false viscountess regularly finds additional sources of income that only occult and unmentionable activities could provide.

Thus, some time after their arrival in Palmyra, the couple divorced so that Marga could receive her full dowry (the dowry system allows a woman to receive her dowry in case of divorce or death of the husband). Legally separated, the couple still lives together, but their relationship has evolved into a friendship. Note that opium was probably partly responsible for Pierre's chronic apathy, and cocaine for Marga's increasing propensity for violence.

Indeed, the "viscountess" has a bad reputation. She is quarrelsome, angry. She is constantly in conflict with the locals and the military, even threatening them with her firearms. Rumors say she is responsible for stealing camels and sheep weaning nearby. Pierre, on the other hand, takes on the role of peacemaker, trying to smooth things over. Marga made enemies who wanted her head. Several times, she narrowly escaped reprisal fire.

She also did intelligence work on behalf of the British, as Colonel Catroux will affirm in his biography written by Henri Lerner. Her son, Jacques, believes that Marga started her activity as an agent for the

British secret services as early as 1922, when she was living in Paris and regularly traveling to London. Her installation in Egypt had been organized knowingly.

Marga often goes back and forth to Beirut where she receives drugs among other things. She also has a new lover, Daniel Schlumberger, archaeologist (they will remain together until 1937). During a weekend in Beirut, her sons surprise her with her lover. The oldest, Jean-Pierre, shocked, wishes to tell his father everything. The youngest, Jacques, takes his mother's side. Because Jacques also has a secret : he is homosexual. Some time later, in Palmyra, Marga surprises him with a young employee. Shared secrets. Jacques becomes her confidant. From that moment on, the mother and the young son will be accomplices even in the most terrible actions. In his memoirs, Marga's son admits to trafficking and murders, which will mark the rest of Marga's life.

Back in Palmyra, Jean-Pierre, furious, wants to warn his father, whom he respects but resigns himself, fearing the consequences on this self-effacing, complacent father. Marga maneuvers to keep him quiet. He is sent to an uncle in Indochina.

Objective : Mecca

In 1933, during a discussion with an employee, Soleiman el Dekmari, she founds out that he plans to make the pilgrimage to Mecca. Marga immediately decided to accompany him. She convinced Soleiman to take her to Arabia (called the Kingdom of Nejd-Hedjaz at the time) by entering into a sham marriage in exchange for a large sum of money, half of which would be paid upon departure and the other half on the way back. She managed to obtain a certificate that said she was a Muslim in order to enter the holy city. She takes the name of Zeinab bent Maksime el Dekmari. But once they arrived, the pilgrimage office told the couple that permission to enter Mecca was only available to new converts after a prescribed two-year period. The plan failed.

Initially, Marga had wanted to boast of being the first European woman to enter Mecca and thus to be able to write a *rihla* (genre of Arabic literature. Travel narratives composed of geographical, ethnological, religious observations...). But the "Passport husband" was not as cooperative as expected and the adventure ended tragically with his death. Marga never confessed to being responsible for his death, but her narratives show the growing tension between the two beings during the whole trip. It appears in particular that, upon her arrival in Djeddah, Marga was afraid of losing her freedom. Rightly so, since she was quickly spotted as a *roumi*, she was locked up in a harem until the authorities responsible for receiving the pilgrims decided on her fate. Saudi by passport and muslim by religion, she risked being sentenced to stoning for adultery and murder of her lawful husband. She is incarcerated on April 20, 1933. Following a trial in which she received the support of Consul Maigret, she was acquitted and was able to return to France.

But in his memoirs "An odd mother" Jacques d'Andurain makes new revelations about this journey. When she informed him of her plans to go on a pilgrimage by contracting a sham marriage, Jacques was worried and reminded her that she could hardly object to the fact that he wished to keep her with him in Oneiza and consummate the marriage. He writes: "She considered that she could avoid the danger of confinement by the promise of money on her return to Palmyra (...) And as I told her that in the midst of pure Islamic civilization she would have no chance, (she replied) Well, I will kill him." She continued : "I have already started to get him used to Kalmine pills... When the time comes I will give him one... modified. Come with me to the pharmacy and say that it is to kill the dog."

In his book, he admits that in Syria it was he whom his mother had sent to buy cyanide at the pharmacy under the pretext of killing a dog before leaving for Arabia. Thus, as she later admitted to her son, she had indeed killed the Bedouin Soléïman. She had used cyanide hidden in a sedative and she had taken care to get rid of the poison as soon as the death occurred.

There are different explanations why Marga could have killed Soleïman. Was it a real fear of being sequestered? Did he raise the stakes ? After all, only he could ask the king for the necessary dispensation for his wife to enter the holy city. Or, more simply, seeing the prospect of losing the expected bonus, did he demand payment, on the grounds that he had done his job and had nothing to do with the failure of the affair? Or simply, it is likely that Soleiman would never have granted her a divorce and, after her failed attempt to reach Mecca, Marga only wanted to return to Palmyra to be with her family. Following the trial, Marga was extradited to France.

In May 1934, a series of articles she had written about her journey appeared in the newspaper *Le Courrier de Bayonne* under the name "Mektoub" (Fate) and in *L'Intransigeant* under the name "Sous le voile de l'Islam" (Under the veil of islam).

Back in Palmyra, she visits Soleïman's family as the custom requires. She pays them a large sum of money to avoid reprisals. Then, while Pierre recycled himself in the breeding of sheep, and adopted a nomadic way of life with a bedouin tribe, Marga spends her time between Palmyra and Beirut where she has moved with her lover, Daniel Schlumberger.

After the East and the Second World War

Her pilgrimage project had failed miserably. But Marga d'Andurain refused this image and, in her book, emphasized the incredible feat that had underpinned the project. She insisted on her courage and tenacity when she was locked up in Ibn Saoud's jails and presented herself as an adventurer. Undoubtedly misunderstanding herself, she turned her life into a tragic novel.

Since her marriage with Soleïman, Marga has lost the name "d'Andurain" as well as the French nationality. In order to recover her French nationality, much more advantageous than the Nedjian nationality, and to get her noble name back, Marga asks Pierre to remarry. Thus, the marriage is celebrated in December 1936. But three weeks later, he was murdered with 17 stab wounds in Palmyra, without the motive ever being known. Was it a settling of accounts following a drug deal ? Was it a revenge from one of Marga's many enemies in Palmyra ? Did Marga want to get rid of her husband, since she was living with Daniel ? The Bedouins were also suspected because money was stolen and Pierre had many business relations with the Bedouins. He bought herds from them and often gave them loans. The murderer or murderers will never be found. Suspected, Marga was soon obliged to flee Palmyra and the Orient. She will never return.

Now alone, she returns to Paris. She works in a sandwich shop, then sells handbags, and ends up resuming her trade in fake pearls.

September 1939, the war breaks out.

Very quickly, she understands the benefit she can draw from this troubled time where certain things are bought at a high price. Marga moves into the house that her sister-in-law Suzie Carpentier owns in the very chic Neuilly. The Countess d'Andurain was going to devote herself to a new and very profitable profession : antique dealer and expert. Marga had no knowledge of the subject, but her fake aristocratic origins allowed her to value all sorts of antiques - Persian tapestries, Louis XV furniture, silverware... - that high society people tried to sell to alleviate the economic difficulties of the war. She bought them for a pittance and sold them at a high price to the Nazis or the Americans. In his book, Jacques d'Andurain, her son and accomplice in all her deals, who became a member of the Communist Party, tells the story. The drugs. The collaboration with the Germans. The smuggling of alcohol and cigarettes. The sale of false passports to those who wanted to flee to the Americas. The traffic of stolen paintings, the tax evasion... The list is long.

All activities naturally implying the frequentation of a marginal and dangerous environment with which Marga had at least one point in common, an absence of scruples going up to a total contempt for human life. After the trafficking, the assassinations, second specialty of a person piquing herself of respectability.

Because in spite of these incomes of money, Marga, true spendthrift, has debts. The Zenobia Hotel, of which she is still the owner, has not sent any rent for a long time.

With the complicity of her son Jacques, Marga had succeeded by use of forgery, to divert the part of inheritance of Pierre which should have returned to the elder son Jean-pierre. The mother and the son, two sides of the same coin had no limits. And if it was necessary to kill to continue to lead a great life ? Why not ? It would not be the first time.

Thus, Jacques d'Andurain gives a rather striking example in his book. One day, in Paris, his mother asked him to accompany her to an old friend's house, where she was to have tea. There, her darling son, who had already killed during those troubled times, could make himself useful and strangle the old lady. The aim was to get his hands on a collection of jewels worth several million francs. Once there, at the last moment, Jacques said he had changed his mind. Back home, Marga exploded with rage. Then lamenting the bad fate that made her enter a family where men are unable to do anything alone and force women to do everything themselves. True words, which were not really a way of speaking. Because, as we learn from "An odd Mother", if Marga needed help to strangle old ladies, she knew very well how to manage by herself, or almost, when she decided to eliminate one of her victims by poison.

After the suicide of her eldest son in February 1945, she was accused in November of having poisoned her 26-year-old godson, Raymond Clérisse.

Marga wanted to kill Madeleine, the wife of the deceased Jean-Pierre (probably to get hold of the few inheritance goods). After being refused by her son Jacques to carry out the murder, she convinced Raymond Clérisse to do it by promising him money.

But Raymond, having remorse, had finally given up and wanted to confess everything to Madeleine, which provoked Marga's anger. An argument ensued between Marga and Raymond. Leaving his godmother's home, Raymond Clerisse rushes into the subway. There, he felt unwell and collapsed. The young man is led to the hospital where he dies in the evening. Before dying, Raymond was able to confide to the doctors that Marga had served him "a truffle with a strange taste". A police investigation is immediately opened. The autopsy concludes to mercury poisoning. For the second time, Marga is charged and incarcerated in Paris. Facing the examining magistrate, the "viscountess" protests. Marga escaped justice again, for lack of evidence.

In his book, Jacques d'Andurain sheds light on what his mother confessed to him a few years later. She confessed to him that the chocolate truffle contained poison. Why this crime ? After agreeing to help him eliminate Madeleine, Jean-Pierre's widow, Raymond was about to betray her. It was therefore necessary to eliminate a troublesome witness who was about to become an accuser. We won't know more...

Death in Tangier

While owning a yacht, the Djeilan, which was cruising in the Mediterranean, Marga disappeared on board on November 5, 1948 at the age of 55. Her body, thrown overboard, was never found.

One of his employees, Hans Abele and his wife Helene Kulz, were found guilty of the murder. Hélène Kulz was sentenced to one year in prison. Hans Abele was sentenced to 20 years in prison, but was released after 10 years for "good behavior". He was murdered 3 days after his release from prison.

Until then, it was Marga who killed or planned to kill. But in Tangier, the predator becomes the game. But for what reason and who decided to put her on his hunting list, that is what remains mysterious. For, once again, the question of motive arises.

In 1947, Marga moved to the French Riviera where counterfeit dollars and opium trafficking flourished. With skill, she managed to earn fortunes with impunity.

In April, after selling the Zenobia Hotel to a family from Palmyra, she bought a yacht named "Djeilan" in association with three Corsican smugglers. The boat, which before the war belonged to an English Lord, had been hidden during the war. The Lord never came back to get his yacht, so the shipyard sold it to Marga and his accomplices. But the sale had never been homologated, so no title of ownership could be provided to them.

On July 4, her son joined her and they sailed to Morocco. As Jacques d'Andurain tells us, Marga wanted to sail to Tangiers to trade in arms and "help the Arab nations fight the partition of Palestine decided by the United Nations". The United Nations had already decreed an arms embargo on Palestine. Marga wanted to "fight for the Arab nations". She also wanted "to do black market : in Tangier, everything could enter and leave without customs: gold, dollars, cigarettes, any trade was (...) allowed". She also wanted to buy cheap gold in Congo to sell in Morocco.

Once there, Marga rented the ground floor of a house in Tangier and her son went to explore the country.

But everything goes wrong. As Jacques explains in his memoirs, he learned that Marga had put the Djeilan up for sale. Months passed and Marga was unable to undertake her long-awaited trip to Congo or to sell the Djeilan. Tangier was not the occupied Paris where she had made her money selling opium to the Nazis. Here she did not have the same contacts, she was not close to the well-connected people in high politics who had so often bailed her out, nor was she the same as she was then. Since her release from prison in Paris, she had been feeling very lonely and anxious; she seemed to have lost the meaning of her life and was only thinking about how to make money quickly.

In October, Marga tells his son that the Corsicans are in Tangier and are looking for her. Indeed, the agreement was that Marga and the three smugglers would share the yacht. But Marga had fled to Morocco with the boat, not intending to respect the oral contract.

During the investigation, Jacques d'Andurain had also specified that when he returned to Tangier after the announcement of his mother's death, he "found the house on Grotius Street occupied by various people, including a crooked diamond dealer who owed his mother a large sum of money, and claimed to have repaid her, which turned out to be false". Jacques had informed the police inspector in charge of the investigation of his suspicions. But in the meantime, on December 15, the German couple had been found after it had fled to Casablanca.

At the trial of the German employee, he told his story. He, who presented himself as a survivor of the Nazi concentration camps, had been indignant because his boss wanted him to participate in the escape to South America of former Nazi collaborators. An altercation then broke out during which Marga d'Andurain fell accidentally but fatally down the stairs of the boat. The body, weighted down with lead, was then submerged off Cape Malabata.

Half a century later, Jacques d'Andurain thought he had found an explanation which, this time, won his conviction. Although it was as questionable as the others, because it was not mentioned anywhere else. In his memoirs, published in 2007, Jacques wrote: "In 2003, while reading, I discovered who had planned all these assassinations, and why: it was an extraordinary character from the Intelligence Service, one of whose aliases was "White Rabbit", eager to avenge the death of Raymond, whose lover he was, poisoned by my mother: She had wanted to use him with his friends Barillet and Grédy to lure her daughter-in-law, Madeleine Leroy d'Andurain, to Paris, with the intention of killing her."

One more version of the mysterious disappearance of the adventuress...

The Djeilan was destroyed in the earthquake of February 29, 1960. Thus perished the elegant sailboat that had seen the death of the amazing woman.

The ancient site of Palmyra was, for its part, partially destroyed by the Islamic terrorists during the Syrian war in 2015. The terrorists used the Zenobia Hotel as a military base.

If the last years of Marga d'Andurain are dark compared to those that preceded her trip to Mecca, it is because they are the logical consequence of an extraordinary life made of lies, manipulation and deception. Excessive personality, obsessed by money and appearance, without any scruples, Marga dreamed herself as an adventurer. Passionate about travel, asserting her independence and her freedom as a woman who never stopped defying the prohibitions of her time, she paid a high price. A complex personality whose only fear was to be bored, she understood very early on that she had an ascendancy over people, and used and abused it. She was a woman full of energy, with an insatiable curiosity, without limits. A destiny in which light and shadow lived side by side until her tragic end.

The "Passport husband" was not as successful as expected and for the author it was a great disappointment. Marga had high expectations of this autobiographical book that could have made her a great travel writer in the line of Ella Maillart.

In her book, Marga despairs of not being understood for what she is. Adventurer and feminist of the avant-garde for some, deceiver and perverse for others, Marga d'Andurain will remain an enigma for most.

"The impression that I felt was formidable; this immense field of gilded ruins, these lines of columns lost in the sand, these horizons without limits, this palm plantation, whose dark green cut on the empty extent of the desert and above all this solitude, this silence, this life which seemed of another world made me understand at once that I had discovered the residence of my dreams. As soon as I arrived, I felt like the child of this strange land..."

"Can there be a more striking example of the pettiness and smallness, the low cowardice of those who follow the routine of a life mapped out the day they were born and their total lack of understanding of fantasy and independence ?"

"Is it any wonder that I want to live in the desert or at sea, far from the rot of horrible civilization ?"

CHRONOLOGY

May 29, 1893	Birth in Bayonne of Jeanne Amélie Marguerite CLÉRISSE
February 13, 1911	Marriage with Pierre d'ANDURAIN (born September 11, 1881) in Bayonne
December 4, 1911	Birth of Jean-Pierre "Pio" d'ANDURAIN in Algiers, Algeria
1912-1914	Horse breeding project in Las Rosas, Santa Fé, Argentina
August 1914	Return to France, Pierre goes to the front
Summer 1916	Pierre d'Andurain is demobilized and returns to family house in Hastingues
November 26, 1916	Birth of Jacques d'ANDURAIN in Hastingues
January 1920	The family moves to Paris
February 1920	Marga starts an apartment renovation business
May 1920	Creation of the brand of fake pearls *Arga*
April 18, 1925	Death of Maxime Clérisse, Marga's father
October 1925	Arrival in Egypt
November 1925	Opening of the *Mary Stuart* beauty salon in Cairo, Egypt
1927	The d'Andurain family arrives in Palmyra, Syria
1928	The couple takes over the management of the Zenobia Hotel
November 12, 1928	Divorce with Pierre d'ANDURAIN
March 1930	Marga officially becomes the owner of the Zenobia Hotel
April 23, 1931	Death of Marie Clérisse, Marga's mother

February 1933	Meets Soleiman el Dekmari, 30 years old, camel merchant
March 9, 1933	Leaves for the pilgrimage
March 13, 1933	Arrival in Haifa, Palestine : Ceremony of her false conversion to Islam
March 23, 1933	White wedding with Soleiman el Dekmari
April 9, 1933	Arrival in Djeddah, Marga is placed in a harem
April 20, 1933	Arrested by Saïd Bey and imprisoned
June 26, 1933	Declared free after 13 days of trial and extradited to France
May 1934	Has extracts of her travel diary published
Summer 1934	Passes her pilot's license in Villacoublay, France
October 9, 1934	Returns to Beirut, Lebanon. Moved in with Daniel Schlumberger
December 5, 1936	Marriage with Pierre d'ANDURAIN in Beirut, Lebanon
December 28, 1936	Death of Pierre d'Andurain in Palmyra
October 1937	Returns to France
September 1, 1939	The war breaks out
February 5, 1945	Death of Jean-pierre d'Andurain
November 5, 1945	Death of Raymond Clérisse
December 24, 1946	Arrested for the murder of Raymond Clérisse and imprisoned in Paris
February 28, 1947	Released. Left to live in Nice with her son
July 3, 1948	Marga and her son left Nice aboard the Djeilan
August 31, 1948	Arrival in Tangier, Morocco
November 5, 1948	Death of Marga in Tangier, Morocco
March 28, 1949	Trial of Hans Abele and his wife
March 3, 2016	Death of Jacques d'Andurain

Publications :

Jacques d'Andurain, An odd mother, In libro veritas, 2007

Julie d'Andurain, Une occidentale d'avant-garde en Orient, Article published on January 18, 2012

Henri Lerner, Catroux, Albin Michel, Paris, 1990

Patrice Sanguy, Le crépuscule marocain d'une aventurière: l'assassinat de Marga D'Andurain à Tanger en 1948, Mémoire d'Afrique du Nord, 2015

CPSIA information can be obtained
at www.ICGtesting.com
Printed in the USA
LVHW111458190821
695554LV00002B/317